ART AND FEAR

ART AND FEAR

Paul Virilio
Translated by Julie Rose

continuum

This work is published with the support of the French Ministry of Culture – Centre National du Livre.

This book is supported by the French Ministry for Foreign Affairs, as part of the Burgess programme headed for the French Embassy in London by the Institut Français du Royaume-Uni.

Liberté • Égalité • Fraternité
RÉPUBLIQUE FRANÇAISE

Continuum

The Tower Building
11 York Road
London SE1 7NX

80 Maiden Lane
Suite 704
New York, NY 10038

www.continuumbooks.com

First Published in France 2000 under the title *La Procédure silence*
© 2000 Editions Galilee
English translation © 2003 Julie Rose (Introduction © 2003 John Armitage)
English translation first published 2003 by Continuum
This edition published 2006

British Library Cataloguing-in-Publication Data
A catalogue record for this book is available from the British Library.

ISBN 0–8264–8796–3

Typeset by BookEns Ltd, Royston, Herts.
Printed and bound in Great Britain by MPG Books, Cornwall

Contents

Translator's preface

Immediately after September 11 – an event that did not take him by surprise – people who had always dismissed Virilio as a pessimist started plaguing him for interviews. When I spoke to him at the time in Paris, where a plan to blow up the American Embassy had just been dismantled, he said: 'There are no pessimists; there are only realists and liars.'

A realist to the core, Virilio will always be the first to make certain connections. For example, others before this have attacked modern art's dance of the seven veils, the stripping of art's subjects and materials down to the bare bones of an insubstantial representation. But it is Virilio who names the process violence, pinpoints the fear that subtends it and makes the connection between this violence and the violence of the battlefields of the Great War, for example, when the first abstract canvases appeared and the human figure was literally and figuratively blasted to bits; or the horrific return to a literal figurative, with Dr von Hagens' real human corpses – of unknown origin – filled with plastic preservative and exposed as anatomical art, at the very moment the scientific community is baying for human embryos to 'engineer'. No one else has traced this twin genealogy of art and science that has had so much to do with the 'routine horrors' of the last hundred years.

Some people react badly not only to Virilio's home truths, but to the gusto with which they are uttered. When *La Procédure silence* came out in France at the end of 2000, Virilio received threats of violence against his person. He fielded questions on talk-back radio from 'art lovers' who showered him with righteous spite. That flak alone constitutes proof if proof were needed of the pertinence of what he has to say here about contemporary art and terrorism, silencing and noise. Virilio does not mince words, whether in conversation or essay and these papers are both. So it is impossible not to take a stand, whatever that might be.

One pivotal dichotomy in what follows needs explaining here. You will see I use 'pitiful' and 'pitiless' throughout, as Virilio does, and have kept those terms even where a more sympathetic English word might seem called for – because it is not. The opposition between being full of pity – pitiful – and being absolutely without it is crucial to the argument. And being full of pity can also have the pejorative sense of being pathetic, somewhat contemptible, as opposed to its positive sense of compassionate. So, apologies to Bob Dylan fans when he pops up as 'a pitiful musician par excellence'. By the time you come to that phrase, you know that 'pitiful' means 'human' in our fond expression, as well as, yes, 'pathetic'. The shorthand is true to form and hopefully works in the English, as in the French, to cover a lot of territory in just a few strokes.

Julie Rose
2002

Art and Fear: an introduction

Paul Virilio is now recognized for his theorizing of aesthetics and politics throughout the English-speaking world. The translation and publication of *Art and Fear* adds considerably to his discussions of contemporary art and the politics of human silence. These are both subjects that Virilio is increasingly anxious about. In diverse respects Virilio feels alienated from the 'pitiless' way in which twenty-first-century artists, unlike twentieth-century modern artists, seem incapable either of understanding the full horror of human violence or remaining silent. Greatly interested in every kind of creative departure, in these two essays on 'A Pitiless Art' and 'Silence on Trial' Virilio broadens his earlier deliberations on the 'aesthetics of disappearance'.[1] In particular, he is interested in re-evaluating twentieth-century theories of modern art and duration, the spoken word and the right to stay silent in an era that is increasingly shaped by the shrill sonority of contemporary art.

Even so, Virilio's questioning of twentieth-century theories of modern art, the removal of silence and the contemporary art that has issued from such premises and practices cannot be understood as a post-structuralist rejection of humanism or the real human body. Rather, it must be interpreted as the search for a humanism that can face up to the contempt shown towards the body in the time of what Virilio labels the 'sonorization' (the artistic production of resonant and noisy sound-scapes) of all visual and virtual representations. Virilio elucidated this recently concerning Orlan and Stelarc, both world-renowned multimedia body artists. Speaking in an interview entitled 'Hyper-violence and Hypersexuality', Virilio

1

castigates these leading members of the contemporary 'multimedia academy' while discussing his increasing consternation before their pitiless academic art that also involves the condemnation of a silence that has become a kind of 'mutism'.[2] As he put it, anti-human body art 'contributes to the way in which the real body, and its real presence, are menaced by various kinds of virtual presence'.[3]

As an elder French theorist born in Paris in 1932, Virilio is indebted to his experience of the Second World War. Resembling the Viennese Actionists of the 1960s he cannot detach his thought from the event of Auschwitz. Virilio is then continually responsive to the most frightening and extremely horrific features of our epoch. It was, though, the Second World War and, in particular, the tragedy of the Nazi concentration and extermination camps that educated Virilio about the depths of human violence. Or, more precisely, the catastrophe of the Nazi death camps encouraged him to respect the human body and its capacity for silence. In different ways, then, Virilio is forging and transforming our understanding of the ethical dilemmas associated with silence and the subsequent aesthetic conflicts linked to the sonorization of the audio-visual within the sphere of contemporary art.

Through offering his Christian assistance to the homeless of post-Second World War Paris, while simultaneously producing theoretical critiques of the dehumanizing characteristics of total war, Virilio gradually discovered his humanism. Crucial to this discovery is an assessment of the aesthetics and ethics of human perception, an assessment that Virilio began to piece together. Yet no simple appeasement with the nineteenth-century situation of industrialized modernization was possible. This is because, for Virilio, it was through the carnage of the First and Second World Wars that modern art, from German Expressionism and Dada to Italian Futurism, French Surrealism and American Abstract Expressionism, had developed first a reaction to alienation and second a taste for anti-human cruelty.

'To write poetry after Auschwitz is barbaric', wrote Theodor Adorno, a statement that Virilio believes even Adorno would now have to acknowledge as an underestimation, given the increasing pace of artistic desperation, the catastrophes of modernity and the crisis in modern art.[4] Spellbound by human violence, Virilio considers that contemporary artists have abandoned their function of continually reassessing the creative practices and sensibilities, imagination and cultural meaning of the advanced societies. In contrast to Nietzsche, Sartre or Camus, Virilio claims that he is anxious to study the varieties of life and the contemporary art of the crisis of meaning that nineteenth- and twentieth-century artists have shaped and the genocide that homicidal rulers have in reality committed. Connecting a multiplicity of artistic, philosophical and political resources, Virilio is crucially engrossed in examining the revolution that contemporary art is presently undertaking through its espousal of terroristic aesthetic procedures and the premeditated termination of the enunciation of silence.

The assaults on signs and silence that Virilio observes in contemporary art were already deadly in intent by the 1950s. For him it is not a matter of witnessing a real murder but more exactly the murder of signs of artistic pity in the name of freedom of artistic representation. Contemplating the unwritten and nightmarish hallucinations of nineteenth- and twentieth-century art and terror, Virilio is apprehensive not to overlook that this was a historical epoch that simultaneously administered the implosion of the avant-garde and the monochromatic and the explosion of nuclear weapons in glorious Technicolor.

Virilio thinks, for example, that the nihilistic sensibilities of nineteenth-century Russian intellectuals cannot be divorced from the grave disarray to be found today in the advanced democracies. Furthermore, twentieth-century art, through its expectation of the contemporary politics of hate, has added to the downfall of pitiful art and to the rise of a pitiless art that privileges hot colours over cold and the sonorization of all earlier silent imagery. Virilio is also critical of the contemporary world of revulsion represented in New German Painting and managed by an art market captivated by annihilation. Determining the sensitivities of today's artists in the manner of German Expressionism, contemporary art disdains the silent pity of nineteenth- and twentieth-century images of the bloodshed of battle. In its place, according to Virilio, as we shall see in the next section, pitiless art embraces seductive TV images of carnage.

A pitiless art

In explaining the aesthetics of disappearance in modern representative art, Virilio characterized its theories as abstract, being concerned to acknowledge that it is vanishing.[5] Today, describing 'a pitiless art', he illustrates its premises as 'presentative', a recognition that representative art is finished. But where do Virilio's rather extraordinary accounts develop? What do such assertions denote? In effect, he is voicing a doubt previously felt by him in *The Art of the Motor* and *The Information Bomb*: that, under the influence of new information and communications technologies, democratic institutions are disappearing as the key locations where political representation operates.[6] Virilio writes of the emergence of public opinion and the appearance of a 'virtual' or 'multimedia democracy' that is not just obliterating democracy but also the senses of the human body, with the growth of hyperviolence and an excessively and peculiarly sexless pornography. He argues that instead of producing a merciless art of presentation, with its live TV images of genuine torment and aggression, its wretchedness, self-destruction, disfigurement, extinction and abhorrence, contemporary artists should reclaim the evacuated space of the art of representation, the space of symbolic yet crucially sympathetic images of violence.

In considering the art of representation, Virilio is seeking a debate over the status of negationism in art. The associations between contemporary aesthetics and modern ethics also permit him to introduce the problem of compassion. For Virilio, this entrusts the aesthetics of fear with the task of detecting a type of immediacy and a system of representation totally dissimilar to presentational art. This indicates that contemporary artists ought not to maintain their concentration on a chaotic and heartless form of perception. The artistic suppression of sympathy, prejudiced by the attack of medical science on the body and its subsequent presentation, presupposes that the dead are of concern only when either violating some existing prohibition or offering themselves up as images of torture. Indifferent to the sensitive attitude to the body, presentational art opens up aesthetic forms that for Virilio are dissimilar to those of the Viennese Actionists, even if something of the Actionists' self-sacrificial and violent artistic practices endures. Taking the poetic truth of brutal reality out of the loop, today's lethal presentational art of scientific voyeurism is powerless to express the actual extent of human cruelty.

Yet, as Virilio proposes, the aesthetics of disappearance also offers a mask to those artists who refuse to recognize its transgressions. He justifies this vital conception by way of his contention that the depravity of contemporary art commenced in advertising before transferring to the everyday craving for murder that also brings into being the totalitarianism of unquestioning belief. As a result, contemporary art does not check mass mediated nihilism but rather assumes that the representational techniques of the aesthetics of disappearance will persist in further debasing our entire 'hyper-modern' or 'excessive' idea of humanity.[7] For his part, Virilio refuses to tolerate an aesthetics that implies the disappearance of every type of art except presentational art. In insisting on its deceptive closeness, Virilio is objecting to a presentational art that seeks out the total destruction of careful viewer contemplation. Challenging the theories of the Canadian media mystic Marshall McLuhan, and particularly McLuhan's concept of an 'absolute present', Virilio advances the idea that it is impossible to eradicate the comparative and the momentary in questions concerning the analogical experience of events. In other words, Virilio has no plans to become a theorist who surrenders to the lure of a life lived in the immediacy of mass mediated despair.

Hence, when Virilio considers the aesthetics of disappearance, he assumes that the responsibility of artists is to recover rather than discard the material that is absent and to bring to light those secret codes that hide from view inside the silent circuits of digital and genetic technologies. It is through the idea of the demise of a kind of transitory imaginary that Virilio expounds his perception of the nihilism of current technology. He judges, for example, that since genetics has now become culture, artists also have started to converse in the idiom of 'counter nature', but for the benefit of the performative goals of eugenics. In so doing, Virilio argues that artists critically fail to appreciate what ethical concerns are at risk in the genetic factories of fear. Virilio meets such ethical dilemmas head-on when he describes his aesthetics of disappearance as a conception that can be characterized as 'pure nature'. This is owing to the fact that, in his view, and especially following the transformations literally taking shape in genetics, culture and science are now free of almost all human scruples. Given that aesthetics and ethics are ailing, Virilio advises that artists show mercy on both, while combating the globalization of the techno-scientific propaganda of cloning, the new science of human disappearance.

For him, no ethical forces or even the aesthetics of disappearance can rationalize a technoscience that has become theatre after the time of total war or in the present period where the will to exterminate reigns supreme. Such occurrences, contends Virilio, necessitate the denunciation of the pitilessness of a contemporary art that combines with eugenics and cloning while inconsiderately and self-consciously connecting to the repulsion of the Nazis' experimentation first on animals and then on humans. The significance of these episodes is established through the fact that they serve to corroborate that Nazi criteria are at the present time the foundation on which scientists and artists seek to establish a new humanity. As Virilio maintains, the scientific formation of humans is today a certainty whose meanings are technologically determined, calling to mind not the natural labour of procreation but the artificial work of scientific creation in which the development of eugenics without frontiers is well under way. Intensely attentive to post-human developments, Virilio has nonetheless realized that any cultural politics that seeks out restrictions to a freedom of aesthetic representation devoid of frontiers confronts a difficult task. As he explains it in 'A Pitiless Art', after violating the '*taboos* of suffocating bourgeois culture, we are now supposed to *break the being*, the unicity of humankind'. In Virilio's terms, then, and owing to the 'impending explosion of a genetic bomb' of scientific excess, the 'counter culture' of nature 'will be to biology what the atomic bomb was to physics'.

Virilio is also anxious to determine how extreme artists and scientists are willing to think and act before making an objection, for example, to 'snuff' literature. This is because for him the impulse to torture imagines a readiness to ruin the evaluation of the art lover, to 'derealize' contemporary art, theatre and dance. Virilio thinks that today's artists are no longer able to ascertain the genuine character of flawed and shattered bodies or the degree of self-hatred at work in their creations. In his view, snuff literature is the gateway to snuff videos and snuff dance, given that pity is excluded from the outset. Virilio is, however, unconcerned with instituting an alternative declaration to that of Adorno's concerning the writing of poetry that will stand up to the barbarism moving within the advanced societies after Auschwitz. To be more precise, he is apprehensive to say the least about a freedom of expression that features a call to murder. Consequently, Virilio questions a political correctness that presupposes a terroristic, suicidal and self-mutilating theory of art. Making links between contemporary art and genetically modified seeds bearing the label 'terminator', he is trying to find an image of pitiful art that exists outside of the conditions of bio- or 'necro-technology'. Refusing technoscientific 'success' at any price, Virilio insists on a cultural critique of scientific experiment, technological inhumanity and deformity.

Such moral and artistic refusals Virilio understands as a thought-provoking enquiry into a freedom of scientific expression that is at present as limitless as freedom of artistic expression. He declares his unqualified opposition to the appearance of a 'transgenic art' that is tolerable neither within its own self-designation nor as the starting point for a contemplative relationship between the species. Exploring the hypermodern 'cult of performance' in a genuine human race directed by the global magnates of sport, finance and the media, Virilio is adamant on the subject of his questioning of a biologically contrived 'super-humanity' lacking adequate ethical procedures or limitations. To be sure, he wants to turn his back on the fashionable scientific and artistic idea of the human body as a technologically assisted survival unit that has outlasted its usefulness. Rejecting what Arendt identified as the 'banality of evil' at work in Nazism and more lately in Pol Pot's Cambodia and elsewhere, Virilio concludes 'A Pitiless Art' with a plea to condemn the transgressions of contemporary art.[8] In 'Silence on Trial', though, he challenges whether all that stays silent is judged to consent, to allow without a murmur of complaint the contemporary conditions of audio-visual overload.

Silence on trial

In this essay Virilio is for the most part involved with exposing a silence that has lost its ability to 'speak', with a mutism that takes the form of a censorship of silence in an age awash with the obscenity of noise. Unrestricted 'Son et Lumière' events and 'live' art exhibitions, for instance, currently flood many social and cultural spaces. Virilio recognizes such occasions as illustrations of the disappearance of representation and the motorized regime of speed in contemporary art that confirms the substitution of the aesthetics of appearance by the aesthetics of disappearance. Assuming a historical perspective, he points to the previously neglected significance of the appearance and imposition of talking pictures or 'talkies' in the 1920s. In fact, in Virilio's opinion, it was in this period that citizens who indicated silence as a mode of articulation were first judged to assent to the diminishing power of silent observation and the increasing supremacy of the audio-visual. In our day, however, the question according to Virilio is whether the work of art is to be considered an object that must be looked at or listened to. Or, alternatively, given the reduction of the position of the art lover to that of a component in the multimedia academy's cybernetic machine, whether the aesthetic and ethical silence of art can continue to be upheld.

Video and conceptual art have been increasingly important concepts of

Virilio's work on the audio-visual torrent of the mass media and the digital contamination of the image ever since *The Art of the Motor* (1995). Nevertheless, it appears in 'Silence on Trial' that Virilio's interpretation of the new information and communications technologies of 'hyper-abstraction', such as the Internet, is shaping new forms of theoretical exploration that are necessitating an alternative approach to his previous writings on the speed of light. For in this essay Virilio also contemplates the speed of sound. As he describes it, the contemporary technique of painting with sound, lacking figures or images, first emerged in the late nineteenth and early twentieth centuries in the works of Wagner and Kandinsky, Schwitters, Mondrian and Moholy-Nagy. But, for Virilio, present-day sound art obliterates the character of visual art while concurrently advancing the communication practices of the global advertising industry, which have assaulted the art world to such a degree that it is at present the central dogma of the multimedia academy. People today, for example, have to endure the pressure of the 'ambient murmuring' of incessant muzak at the art gallery, at work or at the shopping centre. Furthermore, their silence on such matters is, in Virilio's terms, connected with the closing phase of the aesthetics of disappearance that is also the gateway to a new 'aesthetics of absence', an absence where the silence of the visible is abolished by the sound of audio-visual multimedia. However, as Virilio makes clear, in struggling against the aesthetics of absence in the name of the silence of the visible, it is important not to overemphasize the significance of the visual cinematic image in particular as a method of examining the power of sound. From his perspective, this is due to the fact that cinematic images saturate human consciousness and are more damaging than often recognized. Virilio places his hopes in the 'accident of the visible' and the annihilation of the audio-visual by a politics of silence. Dating the contemporary crisis in the plastic arts from the invention of the talkies, he insists that this is the basis of the resulting condemnation of human deafness and the marketing of sound that has given rise to the 'trauma of the ear'. Equally significantly, Virilio is especially sceptical of the insertion of speech into the image, owing to the fact that the art lover rapidly becomes a casualty of the speed of sound and a prisoner of the noise of the visible. It is also important to keep in mind that for him the arts are presently transfixed by a will to noise, a phenomenon whose objective is the purging of silence. For these reasons, as Virilio understands it, the turmoil in contemporary visual art is not the consequence of the development of photography or the cinema but the outcome of the creation of the talkies. Such a declaration in addition relates to his questioning of the waning of oral traditions that unsurprisingly for Virilio entails the ever 'telepresent' talking image and the ever fainter presence of silent reality. To say nothing, declares Virilio, is not simply an act that leads to fear, to pitiless art and to pitiless times, but also to the domination of the immediacy of contemporary visual art by the sonority of the audio-visual.

Implicated in Virilio's final thoughts about contemporary art's losing ground to sonority on account of its immediacy is his on-going resistance to the end of spontaneous reactions to works of art and the continuing imposition of the conditioned reflex action. Virilio's purpose at this juncture is to disrupt those graphic arts that unreservedly rely on the speed of sound. This strategy is typical of Virilio's 'pitiful' artistic stance and of his preceding radical cultural analyses. In *The Art of the Motor* and in 'Silence on Trial', for instance, Virilio rejects the screaming and streaming multimedia performances of the body artist Stelarc. As Virilio notes, it is of fundamental importance that the hyperviolence and hypersexuality that at present rule the screens of hypermodernity are challenged given that they are the supreme instigators of social insecurity and the crisis in figurative art. He understands the art of the mass media consequently as the most perilous effort yet to manage the silent majority through a spurious voice conveyed through public opinion polls, corporate sponsorship and advertising. Virilio thus laments the eradication of the modern 'man of art' by hypermodern contemporary artists such as Stelarc. Such a loss to him is also an injury to all those who still yearn to speak even when they remain silent. Virilio is accordingly looking to uncover within the field of contemporary art the forces involved in the systematic termination of the silence of the visual and the gesture of the artist. By explaining in 'Silence on Trial' that such forces plan to extend the motorization of art while removing the sensations of the human subject, Virilio concludes that, for him at least, cybernetic art and politics have limits that do not include murder.

The aesthetics of Auschwitz

Commentators on Virilio's *Art and Fear* might claim that his powerful speculations on contemporary media are the conjectures of a critic of the art of technology who has lost hope in the ability of modernism and hypermodernism to effectively face up to rising hyperviolence and hypersexuality. His works and interviews as a rule are, however, very much concerned with circumventing the dangers of an indiscriminate aesthetic pessimism. Yet it does appear in 'A Pitiless Art' and 'Silence on Trial' as if he is at times perhaps excessively disparaging of the trends and theories associated with contemporary art and film, politics and the acceleration of the mass media. In condemning pitiless art and the recent ordeal experienced by those seeking a right to silence without implied assent, he is possibly rather too cautious with regard to the practices of contemporary art. As in the case of the body artist Stelarc, Virilio's criticism of his work tends to overlook the remarkable and revolutionary questioning of the conventional principles of the functioning of the human body that Stelarc's medical operations and technological performances signify. For Virilio, however, the humiliation of the art lover through the imposition of pitiless images and ear-splitting sound systems in the art gallery and elsewhere is not so much the beginning of an aesthetic debate as the beginning of the end of humanity.

In the same way, the thinking behind Virilio's recent writings on the idea of a contemporary multimedia academy only adds to the feeling that he increasingly proposes a type of criticism that is antagonistic towards academia generally. One difficulty with this sort of strategy is that in order to oppose accepted theoretical dialogues on art and politics Virilio is obliged to ignore or to engage with them and in both instances thereby draw attention to the fact that his work cannot sustain itself without such discourses. Virilio's dilemma, of course, then develops into that of both being censured for his lack of familiarity with the contemporary aesthetic and political discussions that he disapproves of and for trying to place his work outside of such deliberations. In other words, Virilio is from time to time in danger of staging a debate with only himself in attendance. Forever on the look out for innovative body artists and other multimedia projects that expose the hypermodern condition, Virilio is perhaps wont to unfairly accuse them of surrendering to a style of uncritical multimedia academicism. In so doing he can occasionally be read as if he is unaware that a body artist like Stelarc also criticizes multimedia academicism as well as traditional conceptions of identity.

Stelarc's theoretical and applied technological revolutions in the field of contemporary art also function to transform questions concerning art's power of effect and inadvertently assist Virilio in conceiving of pitiless art and its deafening manifestation as crucial characteristics of the present hypermodern order. He is, in short, developing a stimulating mode of theorizing in these essays, which moves away from that typically found in contemporary art. What is absolutely vital for Virilio is the technological means by which contemporary art has abandoned its passion and sexual force. Conversely, it is important to stress that he is undoubtedly concerned not to characterize contemporary art in opposition to theory or aesthetic fervour, but to distinguish it as a pitiless and emotionless reaction to the disastrous circumstances of hypermodernity. As a result of such heartfelt aesthetic declarations, Virilio is quick to single out the hypersexuality of contemporary pornography as the most recent source of pitiless representations and sadistic ideas.

Given that contemporary artists and specialists in pornography have twisted pitilessness and noise into the rallying call of a totally destructive and increasingly non-representational regime, it is hardly surprising that Virilio senses that he must dissociate his work from what might be called the 'aesthetics of Auschwitz'. Here, Virilio is in fact paying attention to the reproduction and globalization of the aesthetics of Auschwitz in the present day. He thus not only refuses the collective delusion that Auschwitz was a singular historical event but also Adorno's assertion that to write poetry after it is barbaric. Virilio wants to recognize that in video and film, TV and on the Internet, Auschwitz inhabits us all as a fundamental if often repressed component of contemporary processes of cultural globalization. Today, as a result, art, according to Virilio, confronts the predicament first identified by Walter Benjamin, that is, of imagining that barbarism and warfare will 'supply the artistic gratification of a sense perception that has been changed by technology'. In jeopardy of preoccupying itself with virtualized self-absorption, contemporary art, Virilio argues, as well as humanity, has attained such a level of 'self-alienation' that it can now 'experience its own destruction as an aesthetic pleasure of the first order'.[9]

As Virilio interprets it in *Art and Fear*, the outcome of contemporary aesthetic and political theories and practices is that the viewer of art has been converted into a casualty of a pitiless aesthetics bent on the sonorization of everything. In 'A Pitiless Art' and 'Silence on Trial', however, it is not so much Virilio's aesthetics of disappearance that takes centre stage but rather his reconsideration of twentieth-century art and especially its associations with the ruling audio-visual regime of contemporary art. Rejection of the human body or its virtualization, declares Virilio, are the only alternatives presented to the art lover by the multimedia academy led by body artists such as Orlan and Stelarc. For him, these and other artists and the multimedia events they perform disclose their anti-humanism and lack of respect for the body. Virilio condemns pitiless art and the destruction of silence as a consequence of his belief that the mutism intrinsic to contemporary body art shows the way to the terrorization of the real body by the virtual body. Virilio's words of warning to contemporary artists are that to stop thinking about the Second World War and Auschwitz is to forget the reality of the horror of war and the violence of extermination. It is to ignore the responsibility to value the body and its alternating attachments to silence and noise.

In evoking this responsibility, Virilio explains that he employs his Christian humanist critique of war, alienation and cruelty in an artistic and political sense, perhaps as an *aide-mémoire* of a further precise obligation to poetry or as an awareness of the aesthetics of Auschwitz. Hypermodern art is for Virilio a manifestation of a contemporary aesthetics that aspires to celebrate Nietzschean violence while discounting a crisis of meaning that is so profound that it is fast becoming indistinguishable from what he describes in 'A Pitiless Art' as 'the call to murder and torture'. Remember, asks Virilio, the 'media of hate in the ex-Yugoslavia of Slobodan Milosovic' or the '"Thousand Hills Radio" of the Great Lakes region of Africa calling Rwandans to inter-ethnic genocide?' Faced with such 'expressionist events', he answers, 'surely we can see what comes next, looming over us as it is: an *officially terrorist art* preaching suicide and self-mutilation – thereby extending the current infatuation with scarring and piercing'. Contemporary art is then the expression of all those artists who take for granted that today's transformation of the field of aesthetics into a kind of terroristic performance also implies the elimination of silence. As a constant critic of the art of technology and the current attack on representation, Virilio is intensely uneasy about the development of pitiless art. He challenges its claim to a freedom of expression that demands the implosion of aesthetics, the explosion of dread and the unleashing of a worldwide art of nihilism and a politics of hate. Virilio thus looks to reclaim a poignant or pitiful art and the politics of silence from an art world enchanted by its own extinction because to refuse pity is to accept the continuation of war. But, more than this, in the pages that follow, he seeks to go beyond the gates of pitiless art and the prosecution of silence in order to explore the aesthetics of Auschwitz, the source of all our contemporary art and fears.

John Armitage
2002

A Pitiless Art

This pitiless century, the twentieth.

Albert Camus

This evening we are not going to talk about piety or impiety but about pity, the pitiful or pitiless nature of 'contemporary art'. So we will not be talking about profane art versus sacred art but we may well tackle the profanation of forms and bodies over the course of the twentieth century. For these days when people get down to debate the relevance or awfulness of contemporary art, they generally forget to ask one vital question: *Contemporary art, sure, but contemporary with what?*

In an unpublished interview with François Rouan, Jacqueline Lichtenstein recently recounted her experience:

When I visited the Museum at AUSCHWITZ, I stood in front of the display cases. What I saw there were images from contemporary art and I found that absolutely terrifying. Looking at the exhibits of suitcases, prosthetics, children's toys, I didn't feel frightened. I didn't collapse. I wasn't completely overcome the way I had been walking around the camp. No. *In the Museum, I suddenly had the impression I was in a museum of contemporary art.* I took the train back, telling myself that they had won! They had won since they'd produced forms of perception that are all of a piece with the mode of destruction they made their own.[1]

What we will be asking this evening will thus take up where Jacqueline Lichtenstein left off: did the Nazi terror lose the war but, in the end, win the peace? This peace based on 'the balance of terror' not only between East and West but also between the forms and figures of an aesthetics of disappearance that would come to characterize the whole fin de siècle.

'*To humanize oneself is to universalize oneself from within*', they say.[2] Hasn't the universality of the extermination of bodies as well as of the environment, from AUSCHWITZ to CHERNOBYL, succeeded in *dehumanizing us from without* by shattering our ethic and aesthetic bearings, our very perception of our surroundings?

At the dawn of industrial modernity, Baudelaire declared, '*I am the wound and the knife.*' How can we fail to see that, in the wake of the hecatomb of the Great War, when Braque and Otto Dix found themselves on opposite sides of the trenches in the mud of the Somme, modern art for its part forgot about the wound and concentrated on the knife – the bayonet – with the likes of Oskar Kokoschka, '*the scalpel-wielding artist*', before moving on through the German Expressionism of *Der Sturm* to the Viennese Actionism of Rudolf Schwarzkogler and his cohorts in the 1960s ...

ART MAUDIT or Artist Maudit? What can you say, meanwhile, about the likes of Richard Hülsenbeck, one of the founding fathers of Dada, who told a Berlin audience in 1918, at a conference on the new trends in art, 'We were for the war. Dada today is still for war. Life should hurt. *There is not enough cruelty!*'[3] The rest is history. Twenty years later the '*Theatre of Cruelty*' would not be the one defined by Antonin Artaud but by Kafka, that prophet of doom of the metamorphosis engineered by the camps, the smashing to smithereens of humanism.

The slogan of the First Futurist Manifesto of 1909 – '*War is the world's only hygiene*' – led directly, though thirty years later this time, to the shower block of Auschwitz-Birkenau. And Breton's 'Surrealism', following hot on the heels of Dada, emerged fully armed from the fireworks of the Great War where common reality was suddenly transfigured by the magic of explosives and poison gases at Ypres and Verdun.

After that, what is left of Adorno's pompous pronouncement about *the impossibility of writing a poem* after AUSCHWITZ? Not much at the end of the day, for everything, or almost everything, kicked off at the turn of a pitiless and endlessly catastrophic century – from the TITANIC in 1912 to CHERNOBYL in 1986, via the crimes against humanity of HIROSHIMA and NAGASAKI, where one of the paintings in van Gogh's 'Starry Night' series went up in the nuclear blast.

Perhaps at this juncture it is worth remembering Paul Celan, the German poet who committed suicide in Paris in 1970, the same year that painter Mark Rothko did in New York ... But why stop there in art's death roll, featuring as it does a constant suicide rate from the self-destruction of Vincent van Gogh, 'the man with the missing ear'?

You would think the drive to extinguish the suffocating culture of the bourgeoisie consisted specifically in exterminating oneself into the bargain – the dubious bargain of the art market – thus giving ideas, for want of cultural ideals, to the great exterminators of the twentieth century!

Remember what Friedrich Nietzsche advised: '*Simplify your life: die!*' This extremist simplification, in which 'ornament is a crime',[4] has stayed with us throughout the history of the twentieth century, from the pointlessly repeated assault on the peaks of the Chemin des Dames in 1917 to the genocide perpetrated by the Khmer Rouge in Cambodia in the 1970s.

Avant-garde artists, like many political agitators, propagandists and demagogues, have long understood what TERRORISM would soon popularize: if you want a place in 'revolutionary history' there is nothing easier than provoking a riot, an assault on propriety, in the guise of art.

Short of committing a real crime by killing innocent passers-by with a bomb, the pitiless contemporary author of the twentieth century attacks symbols, the very meaning of a 'pitiful' art he assimilates to 'academicism'. Take Guy Debord, the French Situationist, as an example. In 1952, speaking about his *Film Without Images*, which mounted a defence of the Marquis de Sade, Debord claimed he wanted to kill the cinema '*because it was easier than killing a passer-by*'.[5]

A year later, in 1953, the SITUATIONISTS would not hesitate to extend this attack by trashing Charlie Chaplin, *pitiful actor par excellence*, vilifying him as a sentimental fraud, mastermind of misery, even a *proto-fascist*!

All this verbal delirium seems so oblivious of its own century and yet condescends to preach to the rest of the world in the name of freedom of artistic expression, even during a historical period that oversaw the setting up of the *balance of terror* along with the opening of the laboratories of a science that was gearing up to programme the end of the world – notably with the invention, in 1951, of thermonuclear weapons. It corresponds equally to *the auto-dissolution of the avant-gardes*, the end of the grand illusion of a *modernité savante*. You would think it was not so much *impressionism* that laid the foundations for the latter as the *nihilism* of the calamitous intelligentsia of nineteenth-century Russia, with men like Netchaïev decreeing that one had to 'forge full steam ahead into the mire' ... And he was not talking about Turner's *Rain, Steam and Speed (The Great Western Railway)*, the painting that paved the way for Monet's Impressionism.

Inseparable from the suicidal state of representative democracies, the art of the twentieth century has never ceased dangerously anticipating – or at least saluting from afar – the abomination of the desolation of modern times with their cardboard cut-out dictator that keeps popping up, whether it be Hitler or the 'Futurist' Mussolini, Stalin or Mao Zedong.

And so the emblematic figure emerges not so much of Marcel Duchamp as Charlie Chaplin or Bonnard, pitiful painter par excellence, as was Claude Monet, that miracle-worker of a *Rising Sun*, which is not quite the same as the one rising over the laboratories of LOS ALAMOS.

> The new German painting, naturally, represents current sensibility in Germany and it really frightens me. The Ancients invented and represented the world of witches, but the world of Hate is a modern invention, the invention of Germany, spread out over the canvas. The demons of gothic pictures are child's play when it comes to the human, or, rather, inhuman, heads of a humanity bent on destruction. Furious, murderous, demoniacal heads – not in the style of the old masters but in completely modern manner: scientific, choking with poison gas. They would like to carve the Germans of tomorrow out of fresh meat ...

So wrote the great art dealer René Gimpel, in his diary of 1925.[6] Gimpel was to disappear in the NEUENGAMME camp twenty years later on New Year's Day, 1945 ... Thoroughly convinced of the lethal character of the works of Oskar Kokoschka, Emil Nolde or the sculptor Lehmbruck, Gimpel goes on to tell us that there never has been any such thing as old-master art or modern or contemporary art, but that the 'old master' shaped us, whereas the 'contemporary' artist shapes the perception of the next generation, to the point where no one is *'ahead of their time for they are their time, each and every day'*.

How can we not subscribe to this statement of the bleeding obvious if we compare the fifteenth-century *PIETA OF AVIGNON* with the sixteenth-century *Issenheim Altarpiece* of Matthis Grünewald – both pitiful works – the 'expressionism' of the German master of the polyptych illustrating the atrocity of the battles and epidemics of his time in the manner of Jerome Bosch?

Today we could apply this observation about lack of anticipation to 'issues' such as the 'contaminated blood affair' in France and the (alleged) non-culpability of the politicians in charge at the time ...

Without harking back to Jacques Callot or even Francisco de Goya and 'the miseries of war' of the Napoleonic era, we might remember what Picasso said when a German interrogated him in 1937 about his masterwork, *GUERNICA*: *'That's your doing, not mine!'*

If so-called old-master art remained *demonstrative* right up until the nineteenth century with Impressionism, the art of the twentieth century became '*monstrative*' in the sense that it is contemporary with the *shattering effect* of mass societies, subject as they are to the conditioning of opinion and MASS MEDIA propaganda – and this, with the same *mounting extremism* evident in terrorism or total war.

At the end of the millennium, what abstraction once tried to pull off is in fact being accomplished before our very eyes: the end of REPRESEN-TATIVE art and the substitution of a counter-culture, of a PRESENTATIVE art. A situation that reinforces the dreadful decline of *representative democracy* in favour of a democracy based on the rule of opinion, in anticipation of the imminent arrival of *virtual democracy*, some kind of 'direct democracy' or, more precisely, a *presentative* multimedia democracy based on automatic polling.

In the end, 'modern art' was able to glean what communications and telecommunications tools now accomplish on a daily basis: the *mise en abyme* of the body, of the figure, with the major attendant risk of *systematic* hyperviolence and a boom in pornographic high-frequency that has nothing to do with sexuality: *We must put out the excess rather than the fire*, as Heraclitus warned.

Today, with excess heaped on excess, desensitization to the shock of images and the meaninglessness of words has shattered the world stage. PITILESS, contemporary art is no longer improper. But it shows all the impropriety of profaners and torturers, all the arrogance of the execu-tioner.

The intelligence of REPRESENTATION then gives way to the stunned mullet effect of a 'presence' that is not only weird, as in the days of

Surrealism, but insulting to the mind. The whole process, moreover, implies that the 'image' suffices to give art its meaning and significance. At one extreme the artist, like the journalist, is redundant in the face-off between performer and viewer.

'Such a conception of information leads to a disturbing fascination with images *filmed live*, with scenes of violence and gruesome human interest stories', Ignacio Ramonet writes on the impact of television on the print media. 'This demand encourages the supply of fake documents, sundry reconstructions and conjuring tricks.'[8]

But surely we could say the same today of art when it comes down to it. Take the example of the NEW NEUROTIC REALISM of adman and collector Charles Saatchi, as revealed in the London (and New York) exhibition '*Sensation*', with its fusion/confusion of the TABLOID and some sort of would-be avant-garde art. Yet the conformism of abjection is never more than a habit the twentieth century has enjoyed spreading round the globe.

Here, the brutality is no longer so much aimed at warning as at destroying, paving the way for the actual torturing of the viewer, the listener, which will not be long coming thanks to that cybernetic artefact: *the interactive feed-back of virtual reality*.

If the contemporary author is redundant – see Picasso on *Guernica* – and if the suicide rate has only kept accelerating in cultural circles to the point where it will soon be necessary to set up a WALL OF THE FEDERATED COMMUNE OF SUICIDES in museums (to match the wall of the federated communards of the Paris Commune in Père Lachaise cemetery), then make no mistake: the art lover's days are numbered!

This is how Rothko put it: 'I studied the figure. Only reluctantly did I realize it didn't correspond to my needs. *Using human representation, for me, meant mutilating it.*' Shot of all moral or emotional compromise, the painter seeks to move '*towards the elimination of all obstacles between the painter and the idea, between the idea and the onlooker*'.

This is the radiographic triumph of transparence, the way radiation of the real in architecture today goes hand in glove with the extermination of all intermediaries, of all that still resists revelation, pure and simple.

But this sudden OVEREXPOSURE of the work, as of those who look upon it, is accompanied by a violence that is not only 'symbolic', as before, but practical, since it affects the very intentionality of the painter: 'To those who find my paintings serene, I'd like to say that *I have trapped the most absolute violence in every square centimetre of their surface'*, Mark Rothko confesses before proving the point by turning this repressed fury against himself on a certain day in February, 1970.

Thirty years on, how can we fail to feel the concentration of accumulated hate in every square metre of the 'uncivil cities' of this fin de siècle? Go one night and check out the basements or underground parking lots of suburban council estates, all that the clandestine RAVE PARTIES and BACKROOM brothels are only ever the *tourist trappings* of, so to speak!

After having 'only reluctantly' abandoned the figure on the pretext of not mutilating it, the American painter then chose to end this life himself as well by exercising the most nihilistic of freedoms of expression: that of SELF-DESTRUCTION.

If God died in the nineteenth century, according to Nietzsche, what is the bet that the victim of the twentieth century will not turn out to be the *creator*, the author, this heresy of the historical materialism of the century of machines?

But before we bid the Artist farewell, we should not forget for a moment that the words PITY and PIETY are consubstantial – something the members of the Holy Inquisition obviously overlooked ... Let's not repeat their crimes, let's not become *negationists of art*.

To suffer with or to sympathize with? That is a question that concerns both ethics and aesthetics, as was clearly intuited by Géricault, the man who made his famous 'portraits of the insane' at La Salpêtrière Hospital in Paris over the winter of 1822 at the invitation of one Dr Georget, founder of 'social psychiatry'. Géricault's portraits were meant to serve as classificatory sets for the alienist's students and assistants.

Driven by a passion for immediacy, Géricault sought *to seize the moment* – whether of madness or death – live. Like the emergent press, he was especially keen on human interest stories such as the wreck of the *Medusa*, that TITANIC of the painting world ...

The art of painting at the time was already busy trying to outdo mere REPRESENTATION by offering *the very presence of the event*, as instantaneous photography would do, followed by the PHOTO-FINISH and the first cinematographic newsreels of the Lumière brothers and, ultimately, the LIVE COVERAGE offered by CNN.

INTERACTIVITY was actually born in the nineteenth century – with the telegraph, certainly, but also and especially with clinical electricity, which involved planting electrodes on the faces of the human guinea pigs used in such 'medical art' as practised by Dr Duchenne de Boulogne. The recent Duchenne exhibition at the École des Beaux-Arts, Paris, aimed no less than to 'rehabilitate' Duchenne's work, though this La Salpêtrière Hospital photographer was no more than an 'expressionist of the passions' for whom his patients' faces were only ever laboratory material that enabled him to practise '*live anatomy*'.

Already in the eighteenth century just prior to the French Revolution, this confusion of *cold-bloodedness* with *a mode of perception* that allowed the doctor or surgeon to diagnose illness due to the ability to repress emotion – pity – had contaminated the artistic representations of 'naturalistic' painters and engravers. Jacques Agoty, for instance, as a painter and anatomist on the trail of 'the invisible truth of bodies', wavered between an engraver's burin and an autopsy scalpel in his work.

But the truly decisive step had to wait until much more recently, till 1998, with '*The World of Bodies*' exhibition at the the Mannheim Museum of Technology and Work (Landesmuseum für Technik und Arbeit), where close to 800,000 visitors rushed to contemplate 200 human corpses presented by Günther von Hagens.

The German anatomist actually has invented a process for preserving the dead and, in particular, for *sculpting* them, by plastination, thereby taking things a lot further than the mere embalming of mummies. Standing tall like statues of antiquity, the flayed cadavers either brandished their skins like trophies of some kind or showed off their innards in imitation of Salvador Dali's *Venus de Milo with drawers*.[9]

As sole explanation, Dr von Hagens resorted to the modern buzzword: '*It's about breaking the last remaining taboos*', he says … A kind of slide occurs as a result of this Mannheim terrorist manifesto, just as it does with the exhibition '*Sensation*' in London and New York: it will not be long before we are forced to acknowledge that the German Expressionists who called for murder were not the only avant-garde artists. By the same token so were people like Ilse Koch, the blonde romantic who, in 1939, settled in a gloomy valley near Weimar where Goethe once liked to walk and where, more to the point, he dreamed up his MEPHISTOPHELES – *that spirit that denies all*. The place was Buchenwald.

The woman they would call 'the Bitch Dog of Buchenwald' actually enjoyed aesthetic aspirations pretty similar to those of the good Dr von

Hagens, for she had certain detainees sporting tattoos skinned so that she could turn their skins into various objects of art brut, as well as lampshades.

'The painter brings his body with him first and foremost', wrote Paul Valéry. In the course of the 1960s and 1970s, the painters of the *Wiener Aktionismus*, or Viennese Actionism, would follow this dictum to the letter, using their own bodies as the 'support surface' of their art.

Hermann Nitsch's Orgies Mysteries Theatre 'masses', in which he sacrificed animals in a bloody and bawdy ritual, were followed by what no doubt takes the cake as the most extreme case of AUTO-DA-FÉ by any artist. The story goes that Rudolf Schwarzkogler actually died after a bout of castration he inflicted on himself during one of his performance pieces that took place without a single viewer in the *huis clos* between the artist and a video camera.

This is TERMINAL ART that no longer requires anything more than the showdown between a tortured body and an automatic camera to be accomplished.

At the close of the twentieth century, with Stelarc, the Australian adept at 'body art', the visual arts Schopenhauer wrote were *'the suspension of the pain of living'* would turn into a headlong rush towards pain and death for individuals who have gradually developed the unconsidered habit of leaving their bodies not so much 'to science' as to some sort of clinical voyeurism – harking back to the heyday of a certain Dr Josef Mengele who performed experiments we all know about, AUSCHWITZ-BIRKENAU for a time becoming *the biggest genetic laboratory in the world*.[10]

'Immediacy is a fraud', Father Dietrich Bonhöffer declared before disappearing in the camp at Flossenburg in 1945 . . . Well, art is every bit as much of a fraud as amnesiac immediacy.

If *'everything is ruled by lightning'*, as Heraclitus suggested, the PHOTO-FINISH imposes the instantaneity of its violence on all the various 'artistic representations' and modern art, like war – BLITZKRIEG – is no more than a kind of exhibitionism that imposes its own terrorist voyeurism: that of *death, live*.

By way of illustrating the path the *impiety of art* has taken in the twentieth century, let's look at two types of funerary imagery back to back, though these are separated by almost 2,000 years. The first are the famous PORTRAITS OF THE FAYOUM in Upper Egypt; the second, the

PHOTOFINISHES of the Tuol Sleng Memorial in Phnom Penh, where the Angkar – the government of 'Democratic Kampuchea' – had thousands of innocents *put to death in cold blood,* women and children first ... carefully photographing them beforehand.[11]

In Egypt at the dawn of Western history, people forced themselves to drag the deceased out of anonymity and into the public eye – as an image – in order to identify *the essential being.* In Cambodia at the going down of a pitiless century, *the photographic identity of the detainee was filed before they were put to death.*

In the twinkling of an eye we have, on the one hand, the birth of the *portrait* in all its humility, its discretion.[12] On the other, systematic use of the *freeze frame* as a death sentence revealing THE LOOK OF DEATH.

Two versions of an 'art' that French artist Christian Boltanski has tried to pull off according to his own lights in order to fend off forgetting, negation: this *aesthetic of disappearance* that, alas, simply provides a cover for those who still, even now, reject *the impiety of art.*

It is better to be an object of desire than pity, they say ... Once the province of advertising, this adage surely now belongs to the realm of art, the desire to consume yielding to the desire to rape or kill. If this really is the case, the academicism of horror will have triumphed, the *profane* art of modernity bowing down before the *sacred* art of conformism, its primacy, a conformism that always spawns ordinary everyday fascism.

How can we fail to see that the mask of *modernism* has been concealing the most classic *academicism*: that of an endlessly reproduced standardization of opinion, the duplication of 'bad feelings' identically reproducing the duplication of the 'good feelings' of the official art of yore?

How can we ultimately fail to twig that the apparent impiety of contemporary art is only ever the inverted image of *sacred art,* the reversal of the creator's initial question: *why is there something instead of nothing?*

Finally, just like the mass media, which no longer peddle anything other than obscenity and fear to satisfy the ratings, contemporary nihilism exposes the drama of an aesthetic of disappearance that no longer involves the domain of representation exclusively (political, artistic, and so on) but our whole vision of the world: visions of every kind of excess, starting with advertising outrages that ensure the succès de scandale without which the conditioning of appearances would immediately stop being effective.

And speaking of disappearance and decline, note the underhand way the *naif* painters have been bundled away: without wanting to wheel out yet again the 'Douanier' Rousseau, whose masterwork, *War*, inspired Picasso's *Guernica*, think of painters like Vivin or Bauchant.

Why the Freudian lapse? This discreet elimination of painters who never laid claim to any *art savant*, whether academic or avant-garde? Do we really believe that this trend of art's towards ingenuity suddenly stopped in its tracks, *decidedly too pitiful* like that *ingénu libertin*, Raoul Dufy?

It will not be long before the drawings of kindergarten children are banned, replaced by digital calligraphic exercises.[13]

Meanwhile, let's get back to art's fraudulent immediacy, to the PRESENTATION of works that supposedly come across as obvious to all and sundry without requiring the intercession of any form of reflection. Here's Marshall McLuhan, that bucolic prosateur of the 'global village': '*If we really want to know what's going on in the present, we should first ask the artists*; they know a lot more than scientists and technocrats *since they live in the absolute present.*'

Here we find the same line of thought as René Gimpel's – only, deformed by the Canadian sociologist's media-haunted ideology. What is this ABSOLUTE PRESENT (that 'absolute' is surely tautological!) if not the resurgence of a classicism that already laid claim to the *eternal present* of art, even going so far as to freeze it in geometric standards (witness the Golden Mean) bearing no relationship to the relative and ephemeral nature of analogical perception of events. *Impressionism* would try to free us from these standards, on the threshold of industrial modernity.

Contrary to appearances, REAL TIME – this 'present' that imposes itself on everyone in the speeding-up of daily reality – is, in fact, only ever the repetition of the splendid academic isolation of bygone days. A mass media academicism that seeks to freeze all originality and all poetics in the inertia of immediacy.

'*Inertia is a raw form of despair*', Saint-Exupéry claimed, at the end of his life.[14] This goes some way to explaining the relentless desire not to save phenomena, as in the past, but to shed them, to spirit them away behind the artifice of the manipulation of signs and signals by a *digital* technology that has now sunk its teeth into the whole array of artistic disciplines, from the taking of photographs to the capturing of sounds. Things have reached such a pitch that a *pitiful* musician par excellence like Bob Dylan can bemoan the fact that

All the music you hear these days is just electricity! You can't hear the singer breathing anymore behind this electronic wall. You can't hear a heart beating anymore. Go to any bar and listen to a blues group and you'll be touched, moved. Then listen to the same group on a CD and you'll wonder where the sound you heard in the bar disappeared to.

The demise of the relative and analogical character of photographic shots and sound samples in favour of the absolute, digital character of the computer, following the synthesizer, is thus also the loss of the poetics of the ephemeral. For one brief moment *Impressionism* – in painting and in music – was able to retrieve the flavour of the ephemeral before the *nihilism* of contemporary technology wiped it out once and for all.

'We live in a world traversed by a limitless destructive force', reckoned Jonathan Mann, the man in charge of the World Health Organization's fight against AIDS, before he disappeared, a victim of the crash of Swissair Flight 111.

Impossible indeed to imagine the art of the twentieth century without weighing the threat of which it is a prime example. A quiet yet visible, even blinding, threat.[15] In the wake of the *counter culture*, aren't we now at the dawning of a culture and an art that are *counter-nature*?

That, in any case, was the question that seemed to be being posed by a conference held at the Institut Heinrich Heine in Paris in the winter of 1999. The title of the conference was: 'The Elimination of Nature as a Theme in Contemporary Art'.

As far as contemporary science and biology go, doubt is no longer an option, for genetics is on the way to becoming an art, a *transgenic art*, a culture of the embryo to purely performative ends, just as the eugenicists of the beginning of the twentieth century hoped. When Nietzsche decided that 'moral judgements, like all religious judgements, belong to ignorance', he flung the door to the laboratories of terror wide open.

To demonstrate or to 'monstrate', that is the question: whether to practise some kind of aesthetic or ethic demonstration or to practise the cleansing of all 'nature', all 'culture', through the technically oriented efficiency of a mere 'monstration', a show, a blatant presentation of horror.

The expressionism of a MONSTER, born of the labour of a science deliberately deprived of a conscience ... As though, thanks to the progress of genetics, teratology had suddenly become the SUMMUM of BIOLOGY and the oddball the new form of genius – only, not a literary or artistic genius anymore, but a GENETIC GENIUS.

> The world is sick, a lot sicker than people realise. That's what we must first acknowledge *so that we can take pity on it*. We shouldn't condemn this world so much as feel sorry for it. *The world needs pity*. Only pity has a chance of cobbling its pride.

So wrote George Bernanos in 1939 ... Sixty years on, the world is sicker still, but scientist propaganda is infinitely more effective and anaesthesia has the territory covered. As for pride, pride has gotten completely out of hand, thanks to globalization; and *pity* has now bitten the dust just as *piety* once succumbed in the century of philo-folly à la Nietzsche.

They say the purpose of ethics is to slow down the rate at which things happen. Confronted by the general speeding-up of phenomena in our hyper-modern world, this curbing by conscience seems pretty feeble.

We are familiar with *extreme sports*, in which the champion risks death striving for some pointless performance – 'going for it'. Now we find the man of science, adept in *extreme sciences*, running the supreme risk of denaturing the living being – having already shattered his living environment.

Thanks to the decryption of the map of the human genome, geneticists are now using cloning in the quest for the *chimera*, the hybridization of man and animal. How can we fail to see that these 'scientific extremists', far from merely threatening the unicity of the human race by trafficking embryos, are also taking their axe to the whole philosophical and physiological panoply that previously gave the term SCIENCE its very meaning? In so doing, they threaten science itself with disappearance.

Extreme arts, such as transgenic practices, aim at nothing less than to embark BIOLOGY on the road to a kind of 'expressionism' whereby teratology will no longer be content just to study malformations, but will resolutely set off in quest of their chimeric reproduction.

As in ancient myths, science, thus enfeebled, will once more become the 'theatre of phantasmatic appearances' of chimera of all kinds. And so the engendering of monsters will endeavour to contribute to the malevolent power of the demi-urge, with its ability to go beyond the physiology of the being. Which is only in keeping with what was already being produced by the German Expressionism denounced by René Gimpel. But also, first and foremost, by the horror of the laboratories of the extermination camps.

It is no longer enough now to oppose negationism of the Shoah; we also need to categorically reject negationism of art – by rejecting this 'art brut' that secretly constitutes *engineering of the living*, thanks to the gradual decryption of DNA; this 'eugenics' that no longer speaks its name yet is gearing up all the same to reproduce the abomination of desolation, not just by putting innocent victims to death anymore but by *bringing* the new HOMUNCULUS *to life*.

In 1997, a member of the French National Ethics Committee, Axel Kahn, wrote of cloning: 'It is no longer a matter of tests on a man but of actual tests for a man. That a life so created is now genetically programmed to suffer abnormally – this constitutes absolute horror.[16]

How can we fail to see here the catastrophic continuation of Nazi experimentation, experimentation destined as a priority for the pilots of the Luftwaffe and the soldiers of the Wehrmacht, those *supermen* engaged body and soul in a total war?

In Hitler's time, Professor Eugen Fischer, founder and director of the 'Institute of Anthropology, Human Genetics and Eugenics (IEG), declared that animal experiments still dominated research only because we have very limited means of obtaining human embryonic material'.[17] Fischer went on to say that, 'When we have done with research on rabbits, which remains the main type of research for the moment, we will move on to human embryos'.[18] With the abundant stock of human embryos at the end of the twentieth century this is, alas, a done deal ...

But stay tuned to what the German geneticist went on to say in 1940. 'Research on twins constitutes the specific method for studying human genetics.'[19] Two years later, Adolf Hitler made Eugen Fischer an honorary member of the 'Scientific Senate' of the Wehrmacht; he was succeeded as head of the IEG by Professor Otmar von Verschuer, a specialist in twins ...

From that moment, AUSCHWITZ-BIRKENAU became a research laboratory undoubtedly unique in the world, the laboratory of the 'Institute of Anthropology, Human Genetics and Eugenics'. The name of Professor Verschuer's assistant was Josef Mengele. You know the rest.[20]

As recently as 1998, the British medical weekly *The Lancet* condemned the initiatives of the European Union and the United States in trying to introduce a total ban on the practice of human cloning. A year later, the editors were still arguing that 'the creation of human beings' had become 'inevitable', regardless. The editors of the London publication wrote that:

> The medical community will one day have to address the care of and respect for people created by cloning techniques. That discussion had better begin now, before the newspaper headlines roll over the individuality of the first person born this way.[21]

They went on to stress that, all in all, 'there is no difference between an identical twin and a clone (delayed identical twin)'.[22]

It is not too hard to imagine the consequences of this confusion between PROCREATION and CREATION, of the demiurgic pretensions of a eugenics that no longer has any limits. Now that *medically assisted procreation* of the embryo has led to *genetically programmed creation* of the double, the gap between HUMAN and TRANSHUMAN has been closed just as those old New Age disciples had hoped; and the celebrated British review *The Lancet* can arrogate to itself the exorbitant right to remove the term INHUMAN from our vocabulary!

Sir Francis Galton, the unredeemed eugenicist, is back in the land of his cousin Darwin: *freedom of aesthetic expression* now knows no bounds. Not only is everything from now on 'possible'. It is 'inevitable'!

Thanks to the genetic bomb, the science of biology has become a major art – only, an EXTREME ART.

This helps make sense of the title of that Heinrich Heine Institute conference, 'The Elimination of Nature as a Theme in Contemporary Art'. It also makes sense of the recent innovation not only of a COUNTER CULTURE, opposed to the culture of the bourgeoisie, but also of an art that is frankly COUNTER-NATURE, peddling as it does a eugenics that has finally triumphed over all prejudice absolutely, in spite of the numberless horrors of the waning century.

Having *broken the taboos* of suffocating bourgeois culture, we are now supposed to *break the being*, the unicity of humankind, through the impending explosion of a genetic bomb that will be to biology what the atomic bomb was to physics.

You don't make literature out of warm and fuzzy feelings, they say. And they are probably right. But how far do we go in the opposite direction? As far as SNUFF LITERATURE, in which the conformism of abjection innovates an academicism of horror, an official art of macabre entertainment? In the United States, to take one example, the torturing of the human body by sharp instruments seems to have become the preferred image of advertising, according to the *Wall Street Journal* of 4 May 2000.

Hit over the head by such media bludgeoning, the art lover is surely already the victim of what psychiatrists call *impaired judgement*. Which is the first step in an accelerated process of derealization, contemporary art accepting the escalation in extremism and therefore in insignificance, with significance going the way of the 'heroic' nature of old-fashioned official art, and obscenity now exceeding all bounds with SNUFF MOVIES and death, live ...

Let's turn now to contemporary theatre and dance, in particular the work of choreographer Meg Stuart. Since the early 1990s, Stuart has been taking her stage performance to the limit. In *Disfigured Study* of 1991, the dancer's skin looked like it was straining to contain a body in the process of dislocating itself in a brutal vision of automatic self-mutilation. Devastated bodies seemed like so many panicky signs of a live spectacle in which 'the catastrophic intensity condenses a terrifying serenity at the edge of the abyss' – as you could read in the press apropos Stuart's most recent work, *Appetite*, conceived with the installation artist Ann Hamilton.

In work like this, everything is dance, dance involving 'bodies without hands, twisted legs, wavering identity expressing who knows what self-hatred'.[23] After the SNUFF VIDEO, we now have the SNUFF DANCE, the dance of death of the slaughterhouses of modernity.

Whether Adorno likes it or not, the spectacle of abjection remains the same, after as before Auschwitz. But it has become politically incorrect to say so. All in the name of freedom of expression, a freedom contemporary with the terrorist politics Joseph Goebbels described as 'the art of making possible what seemed impossible'.[24]

But let's dispel any doubts we might still have. Despite the current negationism, freedom of expression has at least one limit: *the call to murder and torture*. Remember the *media of hate* in the ex-Yugoslavia of Slobodan Milosovic? Remember the 'Thousand Hills Radio' of the Great Lakes region of Africa calling Rwandans to inter-ethnic genocide? Confronted by such 'expressionist' events, surely we can see what comes next, looming over us as it is: *an officially terrorist art* preaching suicide and self-mutilation – thereby extending the current infatuation with scarring and piercing. Or else random slaughter, the coming of a THANATOPHILIA that would revive the now forgotten fascist slogan: *VIVA LA MUERTA!*

At this point we might note the project of the multinational Monsanto designed to genetically programme crop sterilization and designated by the telling name 'TERMINATOR'. Are we still talking biotechnology here? Aren't we really talking about a form of *necro-technology* aimed at ensuring one firm's monopoly?

Thanatophilia, necro-technology and one day soon, teratology ... Is this genetic trance still a science, some new alchemy, or is it *an extreme art?*

For confirmation we need look no further than the Harvard Medical School where Malcolm Logan and Clifford Tabin recently created a mutation that says a lot about the fundamentally expressionist nature of genetic engineering.

> After locating a gene that seemed to play a decisive role in the formation of a chicken's hindlimbs, Logan and Tabin took the radical step of introducing the gene into the genome of a virus which they then injected into the developing wings of a chicken embryo to test the function of the gene.[25]

Some weeks later, this TERATOLOGICAL breakthrough made headlines.

> The chicken's wings have undergone major transformations and now look like legs, with the wing twisted into a position suitable for walking and the fingers pivoting to facilitate pressure on the ground. The placement of the muscles is radically different, too, better adapted to the specific functions of walking.[26]

But this monster is not yet perfect, however, for its Kafkaesque metamorphosis is incomplete ... The 'four-legged chicken' is in fact an experimental failure worthy of featuring in the bestiary of a Jerome Bosch! After the 'Doctor Strangeloves' of the atomic bomb, voilà 'Frankenstein', no less: *the monster has become the chimerical horizon of the study of malformations.* And it won't be long before human guinea pigs are used instead of animals in future experiments.

Let's hear it from those trying to denounce this drift of *genetic expressionism*, from the inside:

> The dazzle of success is goading biologists implacably on, each

obstacle overcome leading them to take up the next challenge – a challenge *even greater, even more insane?* We should note that if this challenge is not met, the consequences will not be felt by the biologists alone but also by this improbable and uncertain child whose birth they will have enabled in spite of everything.

So writes Axel Kahn apropos 'medically assisted pro-creation'. Kahn concludes, 'Everything in the history of human enterprise would indicate that this headlong rush into the future will one day end in catastrophies – in botched attempts at human beings.'[27]

How can we fail here to denounce yet another facet of negationism: that of the deliberate overlooking of the famous NUREMBURG CODE, set down in 1947 in the wake of the horrors the Nazi doctors perpetrated? 'The Nuremburg Code established the conditions under which tests on human beings could be conducted; it is a fundamental text for modern medical ethics', as Axel Kahn rightly reminds us ... There is not a hint of respect for any of this in the contemporary trials: 'When will the Nuremburg Code be applied to medically assisted procreation ... to the attempts at creating a human being?' asks Kahn, as a geneticist and member of the French National Ethics Committee, by way of conclusion.

Ethics or aesthetics? That is indeed the question at the dawn of the millennium. If freedom of SCIENTIFIC expression now actually has no more limits than freedom of ARTISTIC expression, where will *inhumanity* end in future?

After all the great periods of art, after the great schools such as the classical and the baroque, after contemporary expressionism, are we not now heading for that *great transgenic art* in which every pharmacy, every laboratory will launch its own 'lifestyles', its own transhuman fashions? A chimerical explosion worthy of featuring in some future *Salon of New Realities* – if not in a *Museum of Eugenic Art*.

As one critic recently put it: '*Artists have their bit to say about the laws of nature at this fin de siècle.*' What is urgently required is '*to define a new relationship between species, one that is not conceived in the loaded terms of bestiality*'.[28]

It is not entirely irrelevant to point out here that if 'extreme sports' came before 'extreme sciences', there is a good reason for this, one that has to do with the cult of performance, of *art for art's sake*, the breaking of records of every imaginable kind.

When it comes to the ingestion of certain substances by top-level sportspeople, a number of trainers are already asking about limits. 'We are at the beginnings of biological reprogramming yet we don't know how far we are not going to be able to go.' Beyond the drug tests and medical monitoring that champions are already subject to, the general lack of guidelines opens the way to genetic manipulation and cellular enhancement as well as doping on a molecular level. According to Gérard Dine, head of the 'Mobile Biological Unit' launched by the French Minister of Youth and Sport:

> Sportspeople are managed by an entourage who are under more and more pressure from the media and their financial backers. If the current debate isn't settled pretty swiftly, a person will only have to ask in order to be programmed to win.

'*The assembly-line champion is already on the drawing board.* Soon we will even be able to intervene with precision on energy levels and mechanical, muscular and neurological elements', one expert claims. After all, the German Democratic Republic did it in the 1970s using synthetic hormones, but these left a trace. Thanks to genomics, you can now enter the human system in the same way as you break into a computer bank – without leaving any trace at all.

'The lack of guidelines requires us urgently to define *an ethical boundary that would make clear what comes under therapy and what is out of bounds.*'[29]

If we do not put in place some sort of code that would extend what was covered by the Nuremburg Code in the area of experimentation on top-level sportspeople, the Olympic Games of the year 2020 or 2030, say, will be mere *games of the transgenic circus* in which the magicians of the human genome will hold up for our applause the exploits of the *stadium gods* of a triumphant super-humanity.

Ethical boundary, aesthetic boundary of sport as of art. Without limits, there is no value; without value, there is no esteem, no respect and especially no pity: *death to the referee*! You know how it goes ...

Already, more or less everywhere you turn, you hear the words that precede that fatal habituation to the banalization of excess. For certain philosophers the body is already no more than a phenomenon of memory, *the remnants of an archaic body*; and the human being, a mere biped, fragile of flesh and so slow to grow up and defend itself that the species should not have survived ...

To make up for this lack, this 'native infirmity' as they call it, echoing a phrase used by Leroi-Gourhan, man invented tools, prostheses and a whole technological corpus without which he would not have survived ... But this is a restrospective vision incapable of coming to terms with the outrageousness of the time that is approaching. Géricault, Picasso and Dali, Galton and Mengele ... Who comes next?

Where will it end, this impiety of art, of the arts and crafts of this 'transfiguration' that not only fulfils the dreams of the German Expressionists but also those of the Futurists, those 'hate-makers' whose destructiveness Hans Magnus Enzensberger has dissected.

Remember Mayakovsky's war cry, that blast of poetic premonition: 'Let your axes dance on the bald skulls of the well-heeled egoists and grocers. Kill! Kill! Kill! One good thing: their skulls will make perfect ashtrays.'[30]

Ashtrays, lampshades, quotidian objects and prostheses of a life where the banality of evil, its ordinariness, is far more terrifying than all the atrocities put together, as Hannah Arendt noted while observing the trial of Adolf Eichmann in 1961.

Under the reign of Pol Pot's Democratic Kampuchea, the hopes of the poet of the October Revolution were satisfied yet again, though it was with spades, not axes, that the self-mutilation of a social body of nearly two million Cambodians was perpetrated. 'The murderers did not use firearms. The silence, they knew, added further to the climate of terror.'[31]

The silence of the lambs still required the silence of the executioners. The silence of an untroubled conscience, such as that enjoyed by a so-called 'political science' now disowned by former 'revolutionary' Ieng-Sary who today declares, apparently by way of excuse, 'The world has changed. I no longer believe in the class struggle. The period from 1975 to 1979 was a failure. We went from utopia to barbarity.'[32]

Meanwhile, Tuol Sleng has become a museum – a genocide museum. The sinister Camp-S21 (Security Office 21), where the gaolers were teenagers, offers visitors a tour of the gallery of photographic portraits of its multitudinous victims. Here, contrary to the German extermination camps, the bodies have disappeared, but the faces remain ...

Silence on Trial

'*Remaining silent, now there's a lesson for you! What more immediate notion of duration?*', Paul Valéry noted in 1938, shortly before the tragedy of the camps, the silence of the lambs ...

To speak or *to remain silent*: are they to sonority what *to show* or *to hide* are to visibility? What prosecution of meaning is thus hidden behind the prosecution of sound? Has remaining silent now become a discreet form of assent, of connivance, in the age of the sonorization of images and all audio-visual icons? Have vocal machines' powers of enunciation gone as far as the denunciation of silence, of a silence that has turned into MUTISM?

It might be appropriate at this juncture to remember Joseph Beuys whose work *Silence* parallels, not to say echoes, Edvard Munch's 1883 painting *The Scream*. Think of the systematic use of felt in Beuys' London installations of 1985 with the gallery spaces wadded like so many SOUNDPROOF ROOMS, precisely at a time when the deafening explosion of the AUDIO-VISUAL was to occur – along with what is now conveniently labelled the crisis in modern art or, more exactly, *the contemporary art of the crisis of meaning*, that NONSENSE Sartre and Camus were on about.

To better understand such a heretical point of view about the programmed demise of the VOICES OF SILENCE, think of the perverse implications of the *colouration of films* originally shot in BLACK AND WHITE, to cite one example, or the use of monochromatic film in photographing accidents, oil spills. The lack of colour in a film segment or snapshot is seen as the tell-tale sign of a DEFECT, a handicap, the loss of colour of the rising tide under the effects of maritime pollution ...

Whereas in the past, engraving enriched a painting's hues with its velvety blacks and the rainbow array of its greys, BLACK – and WHITE – are now no more than traces of a degradation, some premature ruin.

Just like a yellowed photograph of the deceased mounted on their tomb, the MONOCHROMATIC segment merely signals the obscurantism of a bygone era, the dwindling of a heroic age in which the VISION MACHINE had yet to reveal the PANCHROMATIC riches of Technicolor ... gaudy, brash AGFACOLOR[1] over-privileging hot colours to the detriment of cold. But surely we can say the same thing about the sonorization of what were once *silent films*.

Nowadays everything that remains silent is deemed *to consent*, to accept without a word of protest the background noise of audio-visual immoderation – that is, of the 'optically correct'. But what happens as a result to the SILENCE OF THE VISIBLE under the reign of the AUDIO-VISIBLE epitomized by *television*, wildly overrated as television is? How can we apply the lesson of Paul Valéry's aphorism in considering the question, not of the *silence of art* so dear to André Malraux, but of the DEAFNESS of the contemporary arts in the age of the multimedia?

Silence no longer has a voice. It LOST ITS VOICE half a century ago. But this mutism has now come to a head ... The voices of silence have been silenced; what is now regarded as obscene is not so much the image as the sound – or, rather, the lack of sound.

What happens to the WORLD OF SILENCE once the first SON ET LUMIÈRE productions are staged, again under the aegis of Malraux, invading as they do the monumental spaces of the Mediterranean? The 'son et lumière' phenomenon has been followed most recently by the craze in museums as venues for live shows, though you would be hard-pressed to beat the calamitous NIGHT OF THE MILLENNIUM, when the mists of the Nile Valley suddenly broke up a Jean-Michel Jarre concert. After the deafening felt of Beuy's London installation, PLIGHT, they managed to bring SMOG to the foot of the pyramids.

'I don't want to avoid telling a story, but I want very, very much to do the thing Valéry said – to give the sensation without the boredom of its conveyance.' These words of Francis Bacon's, taken from David Sylvester's interviews with the artist and quoted as a lead-in for the '*Modern Starts*' exhibition at the Museum of Modern Art in New York, 1999, beautifully sum up the current dilemma: the less you represent, the more you push the simulacrum of REPRESENTATION!

But what is this 'situation' concealing if not the *contraction of time*? Of this *real time* that effaces all duration, exclusively promoting instead the *present*, the directness of the immediacy of ZERO TIME ... a contraction of the LIVE and of LIFE, which we see once more at work in the recent appeal of *live shows*, which are to dance and choreography what the video installation already was to Fernand Léger's *Mechanical Ballet*.

All in all, the invention of the CINEMATOGRAPH has radically altered the experience of *exposure time*, the whole regime of temporality of the visual arts. In the nineteenth century, the aesthetics of CINEMATIC disappearance promptly supplanted the multimillennial aesthetics of the appearance of the STATIC.

Once the photogram hit the scene, it was solely a matter of mechanically or electrically producing some kind of *reality effect* to get people to forget the lack of any subject as the film rolled past.

Yet one crucial aspect of this mutation of the seventh art has been too long ignored and that is the arrival of the TALKIES. From the end of the 1920s onwards, the idea of accepting the absence of words or phrases, of some kind of dialogue, became unthinkable.[2] The so-called *listening comfort* of darkened cinema halls required that HEARING and VISION be *synchronized*. Much later, at the end of the century, ACTION and REACTION similarly would be put into instant *interaction* thanks to the feats of 'tele-action', this time, and not just radiophonic 'tele-listening' or 'tele-vision'.

Curiously, it is in the era of the Great Depression that followed the Wall Street Crash of 1929 that SILENCE WAS PUT ON TRIAL – in Europe as in the United States. From that moment, WHOEVER SAYS NOTHING IS DEEMED TO CONSENT. No silence can express disapproval or resistance but only consent. The silence of the image is not only ANIMATED by the motorization of film segments; it is also ENLISTED in the general acquiescence in a TOTAL ART – the seventh art which, they would then claim, contained all the rest.

During the great economic crisis which, in Europe, would end in Nazi TOTALITARIANISM, silence was already no more than a form of abstention. The trend everywhere was towards the *simultaneous* synchronization of image and sound. Whence the major political role played at the time by cinematic NEWSREELS, notably those produced by Fox-Movietone in the United States and by UFA in Germany, which perfectly prefigured televisual *prime time*.

Alongside booming radiophony and the *live rallies* of Nuremburg and elsewhere, the talkies would become one of the instruments of choice of the fledgling totalitarianisms. For Mussolini, *the camera was the most powerful weapon there was*; for Stalin, at the same moment in time, *the cinema was the most effective of tools for stirring up the masses*.

No *AGITPROP* or *PROPAGANDA STAEFFEL* without the *consensual power of the talkies*. Once you have the talkies up and running, you can get walls, any old animated image whatever to talk. The *dead* too, though, and *all who remain silent*. And not just people or beings, either, but things to boot!

'*The screen answers your every whim, in advance*', as Orwell put it. Yet though the walls may well talk, frescos no longer can. The seventh art thus becomes a VENTRILOQUIST ART delivering its own oracles. Like the Pythian prophetess, the image speaks; but, more specifically, it *answers* the silence of the anguished masses who have lost their tongues. As a certain poet put it, '*Cinema never has been SILENT, only DEAF*'.

Those days are long gone. No one is waiting any more for the REVOLUTION, only for the ACCIDENT, the breakdown, that will reduce this unbearable chatter to silence.

In olden days a pianist used to punctuate segments of old burlesque movies; now the reality of scenes of everyday life needs to be subtitled in similar vein, the AUDIO-VISUAL aiming to put paid to the *silence of vision* in its entirety.

All you have to do is dump your mobile phone and grab your infra-red helmet. Then you are ready to go wandering around those museums where the *sound-track* amply makes up for the *image track* of the picture-rail.

Does art mean listening or looking, for the art lover? Has contemplation of painting become a reflex action and possibly a CYBERNETIC one at that?

Victim of the *prosecution of silence*, contemporary art long ago made a bid for *divergence* – in other words, to practise a CONCEPTUAL DIVERSION – before opting for *convergence*.

Surely that is the only way we can interpret the Cubists' newspaper collages or the later, post-1918, collages and photomontages of Raoul

Hausmann, say, or his Berlin Dadaist confrère, John Heartfield, not to mention the French Dadaists and Surrealists, among others.

In a decidedly fin de siècle world, where the automobile questions its driver about the functioning of the handbrake or whether the seatbelt is buckled, where the refrigerator is gearing itself up to place the order at the supermarket, where your computer greets you of a morning with a hearty 'hello', surely we have to ask ourselves whether the silence of art can be sustained for much longer.

This goes even for the mobile phone craze that is part and parcel of the same thing, since it is now necessary to *impose silence* – in restaurants and places of worship or concert halls. One day, following the example of the campaign to combat nicotine addiction, it may well be necessary to put up signs of the 'Silence – Hospital' variety at the entrance to museums and exhibition halls to get all those 'communication machines' to shut up and put an end to the all too numerous cultural exercises in SOUND and LIGHT.

Machine for *seeing*, machine for *hearing*, once upon a time; machine for *thinking* very shortly with the boom in all things *digital* and the programmed abandonment of the *analogue*. How will *the silence of the infinite spaces of art* subsist, this silence that seems to terrify the makers of motors of any kind, from the logical inference motor of the computer to the research engine of the network of networks? All these questions that today remain unanswered make ENIGMAS of contemporary ethics and aesthetics.

With architecture, alas, the jig is already up. Architectonics has become an *audio-visual art*, the only question now being whether it will shortly go on to become a VIRTUAL ART. For sculpture, ever since Jean Tinguely and his 'Bachelor Machines', this has been merely a risk to be run. As for painting and the graphic arts, from the moment VIDEO ART hit the scene with the notion of the installation, it has been impossible to mention CONCEPTUAL ART without picking up the background noise of the mass media behind the words and objects of the art market.

Like TINNITUS, where a ringing in the ears perceived in the absence of external noise soon becomes unbearable, contemporary art's *prosecution of silence* is in the process of lastingly polluting our representations.

Having digested the critical impact of Marcel Duchamp's retinal art, let's hear what French critic Patrick Vauday had to say a little more recently:

The passage from image to photography and then to cinema and, more recently still, to video and digital computer graphics, has surely had the effect of rendering painting magnificently *célibataire*. Painting has finally been released from the image-making function that till then more or less concealed its true essence. Notwithstanding the 'new' figurative art, it is not too far-fetched to see in the modern avatar of painting a *mise à nu* of its essence that is resolutely ICONOCLASTIC.[3]

At those words, you could be forgiven for fearing that the waxing twenty-first century were about to reproduce the first years of the twentieth, albeit unwittingly!

Under the guise of 'new technologies', surely what is really at work here is the actual CLONING, over and over, of some SUPER-, no, HYPER-ABSTRACTION that will be to virtual reality what HYPER-REALISM was to the photographic shot. This is happening at a time when someone like Kouichirou Eto, for instance, is gearing up to launch SOUND CREATURES on the Internet along with his own meta-musical ambient music!

What this means is a style of painting not only *without figures* but also *without images*, a *music of the spheres without sound*, presenting the symptoms of a *blinding* that would be the exact counterpart to the *silence of the lambs*. Speaking of the painter Turner, certain nineteenth-century aesthetes such as Hazlitt denounced the advent of *'pictures of nothing, and very like'*.[4] You can bet that soon, thanks to digital technology, *electro-acoustic* music will generate new forms of visual art. *Electro-optic* computer graphics will similarly erase the demarcation lines between the different art forms.

Once again, we will speak of a TOTAL ART – one no longer indebted to the cinematograph, that art which supposedly contained all the rest. Thanks to electronics, we will invent a GLOBAL ART, a 'single art', like the thinking that subtends the new information and communications technologies.

To take an example, think of the influence of Wagner on Kandinsky in 1910, when the very first ABSTRACT canvases emerged; or think of the influence of Kurt Schwitters whose *Ursonate* was composed of oral sounds ... Then, of course, there is the influence of JAZZ on works like the 'Broadway Boogie Woogie' of New York based Mondrian, an artist who would not have a telephone in the house during the years 1940 to 1942. Unlike Moholy-Nagy, who was already making TELE-PAINTINGS twenty years earlier using the crank phone to issue instructions at a distance to a sign painter ... and inventing pictorial INTERACTIVITY in the process.

All this interaction between SOUND, LIGHT and IMAGE, far from creating a 'new art' or a *new reality* – to borrow the name of the 1950 Paris salon dedicated to French painter Herbin's geometric abstraction – only destroys the nature of art, promoting instead its communication.

Moreover, someone like Andy Warhol makes no sense as an artist in the Duchamp mould unless we understand the dynamic role played not only by sign painting, but more especially by advertising, that last ACADEMICISM that has gradually invaded the temples of *official art* without anyone's batting an eyelid. So little offence has it given, in fact, that where 'Campbell's Soup' not so long ago turned into a *painting*, today Picasso has become a *car*.

Last autumn, the BBC began broadcasting recordings of murmurs and conversation noises destined for the offices at the big end of town where employees complain about the reigning deathly silence.

'We're trying to get a background of ambient sound', explains a spokesman for the British station. 'These offices are so quiet that the slightest noise, such as the phone ringing, disturbs people's concentration which, of course, can lead to stuff-ups.'[5]

Following the muzak that is piped through shops and supermarkets, let's hear it for AMBIENT MURMURING, *the voice of the voiceless!* After the promotion of domestic consumerism via the euphoria of radiophony, it is now production that finds itself beefed up with a sound backdrop designed to improve office life ...

Similarly, over at the Pompidou Centre in Paris, the post-renovation reopening exhibition, which was called *'Le Temps vite'* – or *'Time, Fast'* – was underscored by a sound piece composed by Heiner Goebbels.

Heralding the coming proliferation of *live shows* in museums, silence has become identified with death ... Though it is true enough that the dead today dance and sing thanks to the recording process: 'Death represents a lot of money, it can even make you a star', as Andy Warhol famously quipped. Don't they also say that, on the night of New Year's Eve 2000, the 'POST-MORTEM' duo of Bob Marley and his daughter-in-law, Lauren Hill, could be heard all over New York?[6]

On the eve of the new millennium, the aesthetics of disappearance was completed by the aesthetics of absence. From that moment, whoever says nothing consents to cede their 'right to remain silent', their freedom to listen, to a *noise-making process* that simulates oral expression or conversation.

But did anyone in the past ever fret about the very particular silence of the VISIBLE, best exemplified by the pictorial or sculptural image? Think of what August Wilhelm Schlegel once wrote about Raphael's *Dresden Madonna*. 'The effect is so immediate that no words spring to mind. Besides, what use are words in the face of what offers itself with such luminous obviousness?'[7]

Today, when the AUDIO-VISIBLE of the mass media reigns, beamed out twenty-four hours a day seven days a week, what remains of that *effect of immediacy* of visual representation? *Media presentation* dominates everywhere you turn.

Struck 'deaf' and 'dumb' over the course of the waning century, the visual arts have taken a battering, not only from the *animated image*, but especially from the TALKIES.

Remember, too, what the poet said when he insisted on the fact that so-called SILENT cinema was only ever DEAF, the first cinema-goers of the darkened movie halls being less aware of the actors' lack of words than of their own deafness. The early devotee of the seventh art of cinematography translated the silence of the movies into their own imaginary handicap, their personal limitation in seeing without hearing what the characters up on the screen were saying to each other.

Yet has anyone ever experienced this *feeling of infirmity* looking at a painting representing singers or angelic musicians? Hardly! So why did the aesthetics of the animated image suddenly disable the viewer of silent films, rendering strangely deaf a person hitherto not deaf in the slightest?

'Looking is not the same as experiencing', Isabelle Adjani reckons and she would know when it comes to looks. Adjani here goes one further than Kafka, who expressed his specific anxiety to his friend Gustav Janouch, some time in the years between 1910 and 1912:

'*Cinema disturbs one's vision.* The speed of the movements and the rapid change of images force you to look continuously from one to the next. *Your sight does not master the pictures, it is the pictures that master your sight.* They flood your consciousness. *The cinema involves putting your eyes into uniform, when before they were naked.*'

'That is a terrible thing to say', Janouch said. '*The eye is the window of the soul*, a Czech proverb says.'

Kafka nodded. 'FILMS ARE IRON SHUTTERS.'[8]

What can you say about the 'talkies' and about the *sound-track* that puts the finishing touches on the effect of mastery of the *image track*, except that they are a lot more harmful than people realize? Must we wheel in radiophony and telephony yet again to explain 'the accident of the visible' that goes by the name of the AUDIO-VISUAL?

Bear in mind Démény's bit of chronophotography in which a man mouths 'je t'aime' to a camera that only records the movement of his lips. We've all seen the smile of the Mona Lisa; here you can see the smile of Etienne-Jules Marey's pretty niece as a prelude to hearing speech enunciated in front of a microphone.

The contemporary crisis in the plastic arts actually started here, *with the enunciation of the image of the TALKIES and the concomitant denunciation of our deafness.* You do not lend speech to walls or screens with impunity – not without also attacking the fresco and mural art and, ultimately, the whole panoply of the parietal aesthetics of architecture every bit as much as painting.

After the *eye*, *mobilized* by the whipping past of film sequences denounced by Kafka, it is the turn of the *ear*, *traumatized* suddenly by imaginary deafness. Victim of the war in which the unfolding of time is speeded-up, the field of perception suddenly becomes a real *battlefield*, with its barked commands and its shrieks of terror; whence the quest for the SCREAM as for FEAR conducted by the German Expressionists throughout the traumatic years of the 1920s and 1930s when the *disqualification of the silence of paintings* would usher in the impending tyranny of mass communications tools.

This bestowing of speech upon images, upon the whirling rush of film, meant unwittingly triggering a phenomenon of panic in which the audio-visual would gradually lead to this silence of the lambs whereby the art lover becomes the victim of sound, a hostage of the sonorization of the visible. In his 1910 tract *Futurist Painting: Technical Manifesto*, Marinetti, after all, declared, 'Our sensations must not be whispered; we will make them sing and shout upon our canvases in deafening and triumphant fanfares.'

The key term here is this WE WILL, expressing the triumph of the will to wipe out *the voices of silence* through the din of those famous 'noise-making machines' that heralded the ravages caused by the artillery of the Great War.

And so the upheaval in the graphic arts is not to be chalked up to photography or even to cinematography so much as to the TALKIES. As a contrast, both sculpture and architecture were able to dream up and elaborate the myriad metamorphoses of their representations – and this, from the beginning in fact, thanks to a certain cinematic aesthetic.

'To command, you must first of all speak to the eyes', Napoléon Bonaparte decreed. 'The cinema means putting your eyes into uniform', Kafka confirmed. Between these two complementary assertions, oral culture has slowly evaporated. The art of speaking has bowed out before the 'talking' cinema and the oratorical power of the political tribune has been defeated by media culture. From now on, what speaks is the image – any image, from billboard images to images at home on the box.

Wherever TELEPRESENCE has taken over from PRESENCE, whether physical or graphic, silence spreads, endlessly deepening.

Having been wired for sound at the end of the 1920s – in 1927, to be precise, with the film *The Jazz Singer* – the cinematograph has not only pulled blinkers over viewers' eyes – or iron shutters, as Kafka would say. It has also, according to Abel Gance, *stymied looking* – before going on to render the visual arts hoarse and then swiftly dumb.

By indirectly promoting the rise of TOTALITARIANISM, Democratic Germany's 'silent prose-cution' promptly authorized every kind of *negationism*. Bear in mind the confession of the German priest Father Niemoller: 'When they arrested the gypsies, I said nothing. When they arrested the homosexuals, I said nothing. When they deported the Jews, I said nothing. But when they arrested me, the others said nothing.'

Early warning signs of the pitiless nature of MODERN TIMES as portrayed by Charlie Chaplin, the visual arts of that historical period never ceased TORTURING FORMS before making them disappear in abstraction. Similarly others would not cease TORTURING BODIES afterwards to the tune of the screams of the tortured prior to their asphyxiation inside the gas chambers.

On that note, let's hear the testimony of Valeska Gert, the actress who starred in German filmmaker G. W. Pabst's 1925 'street' film *Joyless Street*:

> *I looked like a poster – that was novel.* I would screw my face up into a grimace of indignation one minute, then quietly dance the next. By juxtaposing insolence and sweetness, hardness and charm, without

any transition, I represented for the first time something character-istic of our times: *instability*. This was in 1917, towards the end of the war. The Dadaists did the show as a matinee in Berlin and the high point of the programme was a race between a typewriter and a sewing machine. George Grosz was the sewing machine. *I danced to the sound of the two machines.*'[9]

A still figure coming to life, silhouettes, shadows flapping about: the *camera obscura* had already been there, done that with the invention of visual perspective. But an animated image, one that talks, calls out to you . . . This was the birth of a sonorous audio-visual perspective that far outdid what instrumental music had already done for the history of oral culture. Suddenly Plato's cave became the Sybil's lair and there was not a thing the visual arts could do about this sudden irruption of the AUDIO-VISIBLE.

When Al Jolson, the white singer who mimicked the movements of a black singer, launched his celebrated 'Hello Mammy' in the first talking film, in 1927, he was answering the unarticulated scream of Edvard Munch. In 1883, two years before the Lumière brothers invented cinema, Munch had tried to puff up the painted image with a sort of SOUND RELIEF, which was until that moment the sole province of music and its attendant notations.

Similarly, around 1910, newly hatched abstraction would typify the bid for *mental sonorization* in the pictorial realm. Here's the way Kandinsky put it: 'The clearer the abstract element of form, the purer, the more elementary, the sound.'

An adept of the then very recent discoveries in the psychology of perception, this pioneer of abstraction would seek to clear the field of all the formal references of figurative art. In the peculiar manner of the Berlin School's GESTALTHEORIE, Kandinsky would tirelessly pursue 'the right form': a pictorial language 'that everyone can understand'.

It is worth noting in this regard that, contrary to the romantic notion previously expressed by Schlegel, art's most serious drawback is its immediacy, its ability to be perceived *at a glance*.

While theatre and dance – those arts involving immediate presence – still demand prolonged attention, we sum up the visual arts immediately, or as good as. The very recent development of REAL-TIME computer imagery only ever accentuates this effect of iconic stupefaction.

Whence contemporary art's shrillness in its bid to be heard *without delay*

– that is, *without necessitating attention*, without requiring the onlooker's prolonged reflection and instead going for the conditioned reflex, for a reactionary and simultaneous activity.

And strangely, as British art historian Norbert Lynton notes:

> Since the thirties, we have spoken more and more often also of another sort of commitment. We want the artist not only to give himself wholly in his art and to his art; we also want him to dedicate his resources to political progress. For too long, the argument goes, has art been an ornament and a diversion; the time has come for the artist to accept adult responsibilities and to make art a weapon. *Art that does not help in the fight diverts attention from it.*[10]

This declaration of hostility towards the prolonged attention of an ONLOOKER, who then finds him- or herself defined as MILITANT, if not MILITARY – *in any case, as militating against the law of the silence of art* – is typical of a 'futurism' for which war was the world's only hygiene. It could only end up disempowering the graphic arts due to their lack of sound.

For if certain works SPEAK, those that SHOUT and SCREAM – their pain or hate – would soon abolish all dialogue and rule out any form of questioning.

The way that pressure from the media audience ensures that crime and pornography never cease dominating AUDIO-VISUAL programmes – so much so that our screens have reached saturation point these days, as we all know – the bleak dawn of the twentieth century was not only to inaugurate the crisis in figurative representation, but along with it, the crisis in *social stability* without which *representative* democracy in turn disappears.

To thus vociferously denounce OMERTA, *this law of the silence of art*, and promote instead some so-called 'freeing up of speech', was to trigger a system of informing that George Orwell would later portray to perfection. NEWSPEAK, the language Orwell invented in his novel *Nineteen-Eighty-Four*, beautifully exemplifies not only the *linguistic clichés* of the emergent totalitarianisms, but also the crimes and misdemeanours of the *audio-visual language* of the MASS MEDIA and, in particular, those of this *denunciatory telesurveillance* we see being installed all over the world.

While psychoanalytical culture managed to bring artists up to speed with tales from the FREUDIAN DIVAN, twentieth-century political culture would embark on the rocky road of trying to control the silent majorities. TO MAKE SOMEONE TALK would suddenly become a major requirement with the advent of the poll and television ratings systems.

The imperatives of *state security* and those of *advertising* become indistinguishable in identifying trends in public opinion. And so contemporary art finds itself dragged kicking and screaming into this escalation in the use of investigative and promotional campaigns, especially in the United States, where sponsorship turns into manipulation, pure and simple. That is, until the Saatchi affair of autumn 1999, when the exhibition *'Sensation'* at the Brooklyn Museum, financed by *Christie's International*, had the unavowed aim of speculating on the value of the works on show.[11]

Despite Magritte and a handful of others, commercial imagery – *verbal art, visual art* – would wreak the havoc we are all too familiar with yet which has for some reason provoked less of an outcry than that wreaked by 'Socialist Realism', the official art of the defunct Soviet Union … The *comic strip* iconography of the likes of Roy Lichtenstein taking on the noisy sound effects of the Futurist machines, Mimmo Rotella apeing systematic billposting, etc. Why go on?

As for Andy Warhol, listen to him: *'The reason I'm painting this way is because I want to be a machine.'*[12]

Like Hamlet reinterpreted by the East German defector Heine Müller, the WARHOL-MACHINE no longer has something to say about the 'worker', but only about the 'unemployed'.

Somewhere between Antonin Artaud and Stelarc, the Australian *body artist*, Warhol does not so much document *the end of art* – preceding the end of history – as the end of the man of art: *he who speaks even as he remains silent.*

Whether what is at issue is the manual speech of the painter or the bodily speech of the mime artist or dancer, we are now living in the age of suspicion with doubt about the creative faculties of naked man holding sway.

With *the indictment of silence*, contemporary art can't quite shake off the acccusation of passivity, indeed, of pointlessness … The case instituted against silence, citing the evidence of the works, then ends in out and out condemnation of that *profane piety* that was still an extension of the piety of bygone sacred art.

Silence suddenly stops being indulged: he who says nothing is deemed to consent *in spite of himself* to judgement of the artist on mere intention.

Accused of congenital weakness, the silence of forms and figures suddenly turns into MUTISM: the mutism of abstraction or that of an indeterminate figurative art whose victims were to be Giacometti, Bacon and co.

'The less you think, the more you talk', Montesquieu pointed out. Surely the same thing applies to the visual arts. *The more you talk, the less you paint!*

The first thing to go was craftsmanship, a victim of industrial manufacturing from the eighteenth century onwards. In the twentieth century, it was art's turn to feel the impact of industrial repetition – head-on.

Victims of an art that claimed it contained all the others, with television following hot on the heels of the movies, the visual arts have slowly vanished from the set of history and this despite the unprecedented proliferation of museum projects.

The art of the motor – cinematographic, video-computer graphic – has finally torpedoed the lack of MOTORIZATION of the 'primary arts'. And I don't just mean the oceanographic arts or those that have come to light at Thule in Greenland but also, equally, *the gesture of the artist* who, first and foremost, brought his body with him: *habeas corpus*; all those corporal arts whose vestiges remain the actor and the dancer. Such motorization thus prefigures the disastrous virtualization of choreography, the grotesque dance of clones and avatars, the incorporeal saraband of some *choreographic* CYBER-ABSTRACTION which will be to dance what the encoding of *digital* HYPER-ABSTRACTION has already been to easel painting.

The Nazi assault on *degenerate art* would thus be followed by the age of *computer-generated art*, AUTOMATIC ART, cleansed of any presence *sui generis* – an aesthetic cleansing thereby perpetuating the recent ethnic and ethic cleansing in the theatre of the Balkans.

And so, after the SACRED ART of the age of divine right *monarchy* and after the contemporary PROFANE ART of the age of *democracy* we will look on helplessly, or just about, as a PROFANED ART emerges in the image of the annihilated corpses of *tyranny*, anticipating the imminent cultural accident – the imposition of some multimedia 'official art'.

Art breakdown, contemporary with the damage done by technoscientific progress. If 'modern art' has been synonymous with the INDUSTRIAL revolution, 'postmodern art' is in effect contemporary with the INFOR-MATION revolution – that is, with the replacement of analogue languages by digital: the computation of sensations, whether visual, auditory, tactile or olfactory, *by software. In other words: through a computer filter.*

After the like, the ANALOGOUS, the age of the 'likely' – CLONE or AVATAR – has arrived, the industrial *standardization* of products manufactured in series combining with the standardization of sensations and emotions as a prelude to the development of cybernetics, with its attendant computer *synchronization*, the end product of which will be the virtual CYBERWORLD.[13]

It might be useful to note, by way of winding up these few words, that the hypothesis of *an accident in AESTHETIC values* – or in scientific knowledge – in the age of the information revolution is no more far-fetched than the hypothesis of the *accident in ETHIC values* that shook Europe in the age of the production revolution …

What has recently taken place in Austria in the aftermath of the tragedy that has been playing out for ten years in the Balkans proves yet again that POLITICS, like ART, has limits, and that democratic freedom of expression stops at the edge of an abyss, on the brink of the *call to murder* – limits blithely crossed by those already going by the name of THE MEDIA OF HATE.

Notes

Art and Fear: an introduction

1 I would like to thank Ryan Bishop and Verena Andermatt Conley for their valuable comments on an earlier draft of this Introduction. The essays published here, 'A Pitiless Art' and 'Silence on Trial', were originally given as two talks by Paul Virilio in 1999 at the Maeght Foundation in Saint-Paul-de-Vence in the South of France. On Virilio's concept of the aesthetics of disappearance see Paul Virilio, *The Aesthetics of Disappearance*, trans. Philip Beitchman (New York: SemioText(e), 1991).

2 'Hyperviolence and Hypersexuality: Paul Virilio Interviewed by Nicholas Zurbrugg', trans. Nicholas Zurbrugg, *Eyeline* 45 (autumn/ winter, 2001), pp. 10–13.

3 *Ibid.*

4 Theodor Adorno, 'Cultural Criticism and Society', in *Prisms*, trans. Samuel and Sherry Weber (Cambridge, MA: The MIT Press, 1967), p. 34.

5 Virilio, *The Aesthetics of Disappearance*.

6 Paul Virilio, *The Art of the Motor*, trans. Julie Rose (Minneapolis: University of Minnesota Press, 1995); Paul Virilio, *The Information Bomb*, trans. Chris Turner (London/New York: Verso, 2000).

7 On Virilio's hypermodernism see John Armitage (ed.) *Paul Virilio: From Modernism to Hypermodernism and Beyond* (London: Sage, 2000).

8 The term 'banality of evil' was first coined by Hannah Arendt in Chapter 15 of her *Eichmann in Jerusalem* (London: Penguin, 1963).

9   Walter Benjamin, 'The Work of Art in the Age of Mechanical Reproduction', in *Illuminations*, trans. Harry Zohn (New York: Schocken Books, 1969), p. 242.

A Pitiless Art

1   Unpublished interview with Jacqueline Lichtenstein and Gérard Wajcman conducted by François Rouan, May 1997.

2   Gabriel Ringlet, *L'Evangile d'un libre-penseur: Dieu serait-il laïque?* (Paris: Albin Michel, 1998).

3   Cited in Greil Marcus, *Lipstick Traces: A Secret History of the Twentieth Century* (New York: Harvard University Press, 1990); see the chapter 'Lipstick Traces'.

4   The title of the famous conference paper delivered in Vienna in 1908 by the architect Adolf Loos.

5   Cited in Roland Jaccard, 'La Bible du Blasphème', *Le Monde*, 29 January 1999.

6   René Gimpel, *Journal d'un collectionneur, marchand de tableaux* (Paris: Calmann-Lévy, 1963), p. 292.

7   *Ibid.*, p. 291.

8   Ignacio Ramonet, *La Tyrannie de la communication* (Paris: Galilée, 1999), pp. 190–91.

9.   Paul Virilio, *The Information Bomb*, trans. Chris Turner (London/New York: Verso, 2000).

10   Ernst Klee, *La Médecine nazie et ses victimes* (Arles: Solin/Actes Sud, 1999), pp. 204, 342.

11   This was among the issues discussed at 'Image et Politique', a conference chaired by Paul Virilio within the forum of the 'Rencontres internationales de la photographie', Arles, 1997 (Arles: Actes Sud/AFAA, 1998).

12   Jean-Christophe Bailly, *L'Apostrophe muette: essais sur les portraits du Fayoun* (Paris: Hazan, 1998).

13   As for the curious name given to the 'Musée des arts premiers', quai Branly, Paris: are we talking NATIVE or NAIVE art here? About an art SAVANT or an art SAUVAGE?

14   Antoine de Saint-Exupéry, *Pilote de guerre* (Paris: Gallimard, 1982), p. 85.

15   See Paul Virilio, *Etudes d'impact*, on the work of Peter Klasen (Paris: Expressions contemporaines, 1999).

16 'Art, où est ta nature?', a conference held at the Institut Heinrich Heine, Paris, 8 March 1999.

17 Axel Kahn, *Copies conformes* (Paris: Nil, 1998).

18 Ernst Klee, *op.cit.*, see the chapter 'Un généticien d'Auschwitz'.

19 *Ibid.*

20 *Ibid.*

21 A dubious account of Josef Mengele's career has recently been filmed in Germany.

22 J.-Y. Nau, '*The Lancet* prend position sur le clonage humain', *Le Monde*, 15 January 1999. For the editorial quoted, see *The Lancet*, 353: 9147 (9 January 1999). The earlier editorial condemning Europe and the USA for wanting to ban human cloning appears in *The Lancet*, 351: 9097 (17 January 1998).

23 *Op.cit.*

24 See R. Boisseau in *Le Monde*, 6 March 1999.

25 Cited in Giorgio Agemben, *Ce qui reste d'Auschwitz* (Paris: Le Seuil, 1999).

26 *Ibid.*

27 *Libération*, 16 March 1999.

28 Axel Kahn, 'L'Acharnement procréatif', *Le Monde*, 16 March 1999.

29 *Libération*, 28 February 1999.

30 *Ouest-France*, 13–14 March 1999.

31 Hans Magnus Enzensberger, *Feuilletage* (Paris: Gallimard, 1998).

32 *Ibid.*

Silence on Trial

1 'A subtractive colour process developed in Germany by Agfa AG for 16 mm film in 1936 and for 35 mm film in 1940. Agfacolor was a tripak colour process, in which three emulsion layers, each sensitive to one of the primary colours, were laid on a single base.' I. Konigsburg, *The Complete Film Dictionary*, 2nd edn (London: Bloomsbury, 1997), p. 8.

2 *The Jazz Singer*, the Hollywood film directed by Alan Crosland and starring singer Al Jolson, marks the cinematograph's entry into the age of the TALKIES, on 23 October 1927 – the date of the first public screening.

3   Patrick Vauday, 'Y a-t-il une peinture sans image?', a paper given at a seminar held by the Collège International de Philosophie, Paris, during its 1999–2000 programme.

4   Norbert Lynton, *The Story of Modern Art* (London/New York: Phaidon, 2001), p. 14, from Chapter I, 'The New Barbarians' (originally published 1980).

5   'La BBC invente le "Murmure d'ambiance"', *Ouest-France*, 16 October 1999.

6   *Le Figaro*, 4 January 2000.

7   August Wilhelm Schlegel, *Paintings*.

8   Gustav Janouch, *Conversations With Kafka*, trans. Goronwy Rees (New York: New Directions, 1971), p. 160 (translation modified).

9   'Nuit du cinéma et de la danse allemande (1910–1990)', presented by Daniel Dobbels at the Cinémathèque française, Paris, 18 January 2000. Valeska Gert is quoted by M. Fossen in the show's catalogue.

10 Norbert Lynton, *op.cit.*, p. 359, from Chapter 12, 'The Artist in Modern Society'.

11 Harry Bellet, 'Christie's, Saatchi et le musée de Brooklyn', *Le Monde*, winter 1999.

12 Andy Warhol, quoted in Norbert Lynton, *op.cit.*, p. 294.

13 'Quite apart from the suppression of definitely heretical words, reduction of vocabulary was regarded as an end in itself, and no word that could be dispensed with was allowed to survive. Newspeak was designed not to extend but to *diminish* the range of thought, and this purpose was indirectly assisted by cutting the choice of words down to a minimum.' George Orwell, *Nineteen-Eighty-Four* (London: Penguin, 1989), p. 313 (first published 1949).

Bibliography

Adorno, T. (1967), 'Cultural Criticism and Society', in *Prisms*, trans. S. Weber and S. Weber, Cambridge, MA: The MIT Press.

Arendt, H. (1963), *Eichmann in Jerusalem*, London: Penguin.

Armitage, J. (ed.) (2000), *Paul Virilio: From Modernism to Hypermodernism and Beyond*, London: Sage.

Bailly, J.-C. (1998), *L'Apostrophe muette: essais sur les portraits du Fayoun*, Paris: Hazan.

Bellet, H. (1999), 'Christie's, Saatchi et le musée de Brooklyn', *Le Monde*, winter.

Benjamin, W. (1969), 'The Work of Art in the Age of Mechanical Reproduction', in *Illuminations*, trans. H. Zohn, New York: Schocken Books.

Enzensberger, H. M. (1998), *Feuilletage*, Paris: Gallimard.

Gimpel, R. (1963), *Journal d'un collectionneur, marchand de tableaux*, Paris: Calmann-Lévy.

Jaccard, R. (1999), 'La Bible du Blasphème', *Le Monde*, 29 January.

Janouch, G. (1971), *Conversations with Kafka*, trans. G. Rees, New York: New Directions.

Kahn, A. (1998), *Copies conformes*, Paris: Nil.

Kahn, A. (1999), 'L'Acharnement procréatif', *Le Monde*, 16 March.

Klee, E. (1999), *La Médecine nazie et ses victimes*, Arles: Solin/Actes Sud.

Lynton, N. (2001), *The Story of Modern Art*, London/New York: Phaidon.

Marcus, G. (1990), *Lipstick Traces: A Secret History of the Twentieth Century*, New York: Harvard University Press.

Nau, J.-Y. (1999), 'The Lancet prend position sur le clonage humain', Le Monde, 15 January.

Orwell, G. (1989), Nineteen-Eighty-Four, London: Penguin.

Ramonet, I. (1999), La Tyrannie de la communication, Paris: Galilée.

Ringlet, G. (1998), L'Evangile d'un libre-penseur: Dieu serait-il laïque? Paris: Albin Michel.

Saint-Exupéry, A. de (1982), Pilote de guerre, Paris: Gallimard.

Virilio, P. (1991), The Aesthetics of Disappearance, trans. P. Beitchman, New York: SemioText(e).

Virilio, P. (1995), The Art of the Motor, trans. J. Rose, Minneapolis: University of Minnesota Press.

Virilio, P. (1999), Etudes d'impact, Paris: Expressions Contemporaines.

Virilio, P. (2000), The Information Bomb, trans. C. Turner, London/New York: Verso.

Zurbrugg, N. (2001), 'Hyperviolence and Hypersexuality: Paul Virilio Interviewed by Nicholas Zurbrugg', trans. N. Zurbrugg, Eyeline, 45 (autumn/winter), pp. 10–13.

Index

CPSIA information can be obtained
at www.ICGtesting.com
Printed in the USA
LVHW051938150122
708681LV00020B/2031